Front cover: Sunset in Trinidad

Below: Vintage American cars are a regular
sight on the streets of Cuba

# TOP 10 ATTRACTIONS

**Beaches.** Beautiful white-sand beaches abound, from Varadero to Playa Esmeralda, Playa Ancón to Cayo Largo.

**Music.** In various traditional styles, live music can be heard all over the island. See page 85.

**Baracoa.** A picturesque coastal town in the far east of Cuba. See page 82.

**Plaza de la Catedral.** An impressive stage set at the heart of the Old City of Havana. See page 29.

**Camagüey.** The streets and squares of Cuba's third city have been restored to their former glory. See page 68.

**El Morro.** Santiago's well preserved fort. See page 79.

**Casa Museo de Ernest Hemingway.** Where things remain just as the author left them. See page 47.

**Viñales Valley.** Visit tobacco fields and mogotes. See page 50.

**Trinidad.** Frozen in time, this city is an enchanting colonial gem and a World Heritage site. See page 62.

**The Prado.** Grand old buildings flank the loveliest avenue in Old Havana. See page 39.

# A PERFECT DAY

### 8.00am  Breakfast

Fortify yourself for the day ahead with a good breakfast at your hotel or *casa particular*. Tuck into tropical fruits, such as mango, papaya or guava, sliced or juiced, followed by eggs, bread and local honey or jam.

### 11.30am  Plaza de Armas to Plaza Vieja

Walk to the Plaza de Armas, stroll round the second-hand book market and visit the Museo de la Ciudad. Head down Calle Oficios, taking in the car museum, to Plaza San Francisco and on to the beautifully restored Plaza Vieja.

### 11.00am  Cathedral

Visit the Cathedral where Columbus' bones once resided and have coffee at El Patio restaurant in the Plaza, a magnificent colonial square with street entertainers.

### 1.00pm  Lunch

On the southwestern corner of Plaza Vieja is a restaurant and bar, Cervecería Taberna de la Muralla, which has its own organic microbrewery. A cold beer here is very refreshing and you can sit outside in the square to enjoy the view or relax inside and admire the copper brewing tanks.

### 9.00am  Parque Central and Capitolio

Start your day at the centre around the Parque. Admire the magnificent Gran Teatro, the Hotel Inglaterra and the imposing Capitolio. Just behind here, visit the Partagás cigar factory, and take a guided tour of the production process of this iconic Cuban industry.

# IN HAVANA

**4.00pm** **Casa de la Música Galiano**

From the Parque Central, walk five blocks down Neptuno to Galiano, where you'll be able to catch a performance (5–10pm) at this live-music venue, with bars, a huge dance floor and a well-stocked music shop.

**2.00pm** **Bus tour**

Return to the Parque Central to hop on the HabanaBusTour, which runs all day. One route gives you a circuit of Vedado, the Plaza de la Revolución and Old Havana, while another takes you out past the fortresses to Playas del Este. The third route links Marina Hemingway with Plaza de la Revolución. You can get off at any stop and rejoin another bus later.

**10.00pm** **On the town**

Get a taxi to Vedado for a great evening of jazz. At La Zorra y el Cuervo, Avenida 23, between N and O streets, the entrance is through a red British telephone box. If you want a table, get there before 11pm when things start to hot up. This is a popular place with top class jazz musicians and the crowd shows its appreciation.

**8.00pm** **Dinner**

While in Centro Habana, you can get a memorable meal at one of several *paladares*, such as La Guarida (see page 108), advance booking essential. Service is leisurely, enabling you to linger until the nightlife gets going.

# CONTENTS

# INTRODUCTION

The largest island in the Caribbean, Cuba is blessed with pristine beaches along the north coast, fascinating old cities with architectural styles ranging from baroque colonial through Art Deco to Soviet concrete blocks, a range of Latin music styles all with hip-swivelling rhythms, a surfeit of rum and the world's finest hand-rolled cigars.

For much of the 20th century, Cuba occupied a leading role on the world stage wholly disproportionate to its small size and lack of economic clout. From the overthrow of the dictator Fulgencio Batista at the end of 1958 to Fidel Castro's tenacious hold on power and declarations of socialism, this small Caribbean nation has assumed near-mythical status as a living laboratory of social experimentation, political defiance and a people's perseverance.

## Legacy of the Revolution

For nearly half a century a combative Fidel Castro weathered the opposition of the US government and the hostility of Cuban exiles in Miami. His successor, his brother Raúl, continues his legacy with a few modifications. The Cuban people have been required to make repeated sacrifices in the face of the American trade embargo and the collapse of the Soviet Union with its support and trade. Cuba is still standing, and despite the hardships has even managed to restore many of its fine colonial buildings.

As one of the last Communist hold-outs in the world, this nation is an enduring curiosity. With much of the rest of the planet racing ahead at a dizzying digital pace, Cuba crawls along in slow-motion, with only a minority having access to

Cuban women in colourful outfits

the internet. Behemoth vintage American cars from the 1940s
and 1950s, patched and propped up, lumber down the streets
of dimly lit cities. In rural areas cars give way to oxen-led carts,
horse-drawn buses, Chinese bicycles and pedicabs. Houses
are furnished with antiques and family heirlooms as everyday
furniture, lit by energy-saving light bulbs to keep costs down.

Cuba is inseparable from the international politics of the
latter half of the 20th century. Children are sworn in at the
age of six to become Young Communist Pioneers. Throughout
the country giant billboards function like pep talks from the
government, proclaiming '*Socialismo o Muerte*' ('Socialism or
Death') and '*Viva la Revolución*' ('Long Live the Revolution').
Portraits of Che Guevara, the 1960s revolutionary martyr, are
plastered on the walls of shops, offices and homes.

## Cuban Reality

Everything has always creaked and spluttered in hard-pressed
Communist Cuba. The economy thrives or falters in line
with world trends, hampered additionally by the US trade
embargo and hurricane damage. Many families continue to

### The Face of Cuba

Cuba's 11 million people have a distinctively mixed heritage that reflects the twists and turns of the island's history. The first black slaves
were brought over in the early 16th century to replace an indigenous
population that was being wiped out (see page 14). But immigration
from Spain did not start in earnest until the late 18th century, when the
sugar industry boomed. Plantation owners – both local Spanish as well
as French immigrants from Haiti – brought thousands of slaves from
West Africa, who were supplemented by Chinese labourers after slavery was abolished in 1886. During the last 200 years the various ethnic
groups have interbred and today most Cubans are *mulatos* (mixed race).

live in overcrowded conditions in run-down housing, and most people earn less than the equivalent of US$25 a month.

In the early 1990s Castro needed to reorganise the economy after the collapse of the Eastern Bloc which had formerly subsidised Cuba. In 1993 it became legal for Cubans to hold US currency. Much of the economy was given over to the almighty dollar, with many products and foodstuffs available only

Factory worker in Baracoa

in dollar stores. Cubans with family members abroad who could send remittances, or with jobs in foreign businesses or tourism which provided tips or wages in US currency, soon had the advantage over those with no access to dollars. A decade later there was a deepening split between the haves and have-nots and Castro was forced to take action to halt the division. All foreign currency now has to be exchanged for *pesos convertibles* and there is a steep tax on converting US dollars.

The glaring deficiencies of the Cuban economy and needs of the Cuban people are impossible to ignore. Cubans also enjoy no real freedom of speech, freedom of the press or freedom to travel outside the country, although Raúl is relaxing some restrictions. Still, one doesn't see the heart-wrenching poverty in Cuba common in places like Bangladesh, India and other parts of Latin America. Housing is provided by the state – you are unlikely to see homeless people sleeping on the streets anywhere in Cuba – and while Cubans don't get nearly enough with their ration books, they have something to eat. All Cubans

School children in Havana

are entitled to free health care, and education is free and available to all. Average life expectancy rose from 57 years in 1958 to 79 years in 2014 – the 38th highest in the world, while its infant mortality rates are better than those of the USA and some EU countries.

Cuba's dilapidation, poverty and restrictions only serve to highlight the indomitable spirit of the Cuban people. They are blessed with a remarkable resilience, forbearance and joy that no economic hardship seems capable of diminishing. Cubans are as hospitable a people as you'll find, inviting visitors into their cramped homes given half a chance. Everywhere there are bubbly school children – outfitted in identical uniforms – racing around the streets, playing pick-up games of stickball, or amusing themselves with improvised skateboards and kites.

## Paradise Island

In dire need of hard currency, Cuba embraced tourism, which has now surpassed the sugar industry to become the country's top revenue earner. It's obvious why, for many Cuba is primarily an idyllic sun-and-sea bolt-hole. The white sandy beaches are dazzling, with the long shores of Varadero in the north perhaps the best known. Other stars of Cuban beach tourism include Guardalavaca, Playa Esmeralda, and the islands of Cayo Largo and Cayo Coco. Amateur sailors appreciate the countless natural harbours, anglers search for marlin off the coast, while scuba divers explore coral reefs and sunken wrecks.

Most travellers opt for package tours, but Cuba's diversity of attractions tempts a large number of independent travellers away from the sea and sand. In the island's eastern corner is Cuba's highest mountain range, the Sierra Maestra (up to 1,974m/6,476ft), site of many uprisings; to the west, in Pinar del Río province, is the verdant Viñales Valley with its huge *mogotes*, limestone rocks up to 400m (1,300ft) high; and central Cuba has the lush Sierra del Escambray mountains and the old sugar-cane plantations of the Valle de los Ingenios.

Then there are the towns and cities. Havana combines fine Spanish colonial architecture, vibrant street life and a range of cultural opportunities; Trinidad, a gorgeous colonial-era gem, its town houses, churches and other fine buildings set on winding, cobblestone streets; and Santiago de Cuba, a colourful Cuban cocktail of Spanish, French and African cultures.

Holiday-makers on the beach in Varadero

# A BRIEF HISTORY

When Christopher Columbus disembarked on eastern Cuba on 27 October 1492, he penned a note exclaiming that the land was 'the most lovely that eyes have ever seen'. Indigenous groups including the Ciboney from Central and South America had lived on the island since at least 3500 BC.

In 1511 Diego Velázquez sailed from neighbouring Hispaniola with some 300 conquistadors. Baracoa became the first of seven settlements across Cuba. Velázquez and his followers enslaved the native peoples and in the process exposed them to European diseases. Entire villages committed suicide, and by the mid-1500s the native population had declined from over 150,000 to just 3,000.

El Morro fort, Havana

## Piracy and Trade

Until the end of the 16th century, Cuba remained a fairly insignificant Spanish colony. The port cities of Havana and Santiago de Cuba were heavily fortified to defend against French and English pirate raids.

From the 17th century Havana became increasingly significant as a stopover point for treasure fleets. In 1762 British forces captured the city. They held it for only a year before returning it to

Spain in exchange for Florida, but during this period trade was opened up to additional markets, notably the North American colonies. A lucrative tobacco industry had taken hold in Cuba, and after 1763 the sugar industry skyrocketed. Though settlers brought the first African slaves to Cuba in the early 1500s, hundreds of thousands of African slaves were imported in the late 18th and early 19th centuries to meet the demands of the plantation industry.

## Sugar island

By the middle of the 19th century, Cuba produced a third of the world's sugar and was considered one of the most valuable colonies in the world. Half a million slaves – nearly half the population – worked the plantations, and at least 3,500 trading ships visited Cuba annually.

## The Road to Independence

Spaniards born and raised in Cuba, known as *criollos* (creoles), managed the sugar-cane plantations but were excluded from the running of the country by Spain. During the 19th century some *criollos* (particularly in Oriente, the island's poorer, eastern region) became increasingly disenchanted and desired greater autonomy. On 10 October 1868 Carlos Manuel de Céspedes, a *criollo* plantation owner, issued a call for independence and liberated the slaves from his estate, La Demajagua. During the subsequent Ten Years' War (1868–78) 50,000 Cubans – including Céspedes – and more than 200,000 Spanish lost their lives. Cuba remained a colony of Spain, but the war contributed to the abolition of slavery on the island in 1886 and cemented national consciousness.

In 1895 José Martí, Cuba's most venerated patriot, led the next and most important uprising against Spain. Born in 1853 and exiled at 18 for his political views, Martí became a journalist and poet. From exile in the United States he argued for Cuban independence. Martí was killed in an ambush during the War of Independence, which began in 1895 and in which some 300,000 Cubans lost their lives.

Throughout the 19th century, the United States, which was keenly interested in the island's strategic significance and its sugar market, had become increasingly involved in Cuban affairs. A US purchase of the island from Spain had long been on the agenda, even though Martí had warned of the dangers of becoming a satellite of the United States ('I know the Monster, because I have lived in its lair,' he wrote).

In February 1898 the USS Maine was sunk in Havana's harbour, killing all 260 crew members. Although it was most likely caused by an accidental explosion, the United States used the sinking as

José Martí Memorial in Havana

a pretext to declare war. US victory in the Spanish-American War came swiftly, with Spain surrendering its claim to the island. A US provisional military government lasted until 1902, when Cuba became an independent republic. But the country was still subject to US military intervention – as a result of the Platt Amendment to the Cuban constitution – which many claim crippled true independence.

## False Independence

For the next five decades the United States, the largest importer of Cuban sugar, dominated the island's economy and largely controlled its political processes. The period was rife with political corruption, violence and terrorism. After 1933 Fulgencio Batista, though only a sergeant, controlled the strings of power through a series of puppet presidents before winning the presidency outright in 1940. He retired in 1944 but returned by staging a military coup in 1952. His dictatorship made it possible for him to invest some $300 million abroad by 1959.

Since the 1920s disillusionment with the nascent republic with its clear dependence on the United States and its lack of political probity or social equality – had grown steadily. Although Cuba had the second-highest per capita income in Latin America, prosperity did not filter down from the upper classes. In fact, the World Bank in 1950 declared as many as 60 percent of Cubans undernourished. In Havana there was a greater concentration of millionaires than anywhere else in Central or South America, and the capital was dubbed 'an off-shore Las Vegas' for its brothels, casinos and gangsters.

## The Road to Revolution

On 26 July 1953, rebels attacked the Moncada Barracks in Santiago de Cuba. The assault failed, but it thrust into the limelight its young leader, Fidel Castro. Castro was imprisoned and put on trial in a closed hearing; his legendary two-hour defence speech, later published as *History Will Absolve Me*, became a revolutionary manifesto. Castro was incarcerated on the Isle of Pines (now called the Isla de la Juventud) until May 1955, when Batista granted an amnesty to political prisoners.

Castro then fled to Mexico. The following year he returned to southeastern Cuba with a force of 81 guerrillas (including Che Guevara) crammed onto a small yacht, the *Granma*. Only 15 reached the Sierra Maestra mountains safely. Incredibly, from such inauspicious beginnings the so-called '26 of July Movement' grew into a serious guerrilla army, aided in no small part by local peasants who were promised land reform.

Following a disastrous offensive by government troops on the rebels' mountain strongholds in 1958, and the capture of Santa Clara by Che Guevara and his men on 30 December, on 1 January 1959 Batista fled the country. The *barbudos* (the bearded ones) triumphantly entered Santiago, then marched into Havana one week later.

## Che and Fidel: Brothers in Revolution

Ernesto 'Che' Guevara (*che* meaning 'mate' or 'buddy' in Argentine slang) is the official poster boy and martyr of the Cuban Revolution, idolised by Cubans. His dramatic, beret-topped visage is seen on billboards and photographs throughout Cuba. Born in 1928 in Argentina, Guevara trained as a doctor before embarking on nomadic treks through South and Central America with a pile of Marxist literature in his rucksack. He met Castro in Mexico in 1955 and for the next 10 years was Castro's right-hand man, as a guerrilla in the mountains then as director of the national bank (signing bills as, simply, 'Che'), minister of industry, and minister of the economy. In 1965, he abandoned Cuba for new causes. He was killed trying to foment revolt in Bolivia in 1967.

Fidel Castro – for 49 years the president of Cuba, secretary-general of its Communist Party, and commander-in-chief of its armed forces – was born in 1926 and trained as a lawyer at the University of Havana. The world's youngest leader in 1959, Castro defied all expectations to become one of the longest-serving heads of state on the planet. Fidel, as he is known to all, was a towering but frustrating patriarchal figure to Cubans. Yet he remained, above all, El Comandante.

In 1985, Fidel quit smoking cigars, saying they were great for the Cuban economy 'but not so great for my health'. In 2006, aged 80, he had to temporarily hand over power to his brother Raúl while undergoing abdominal surgery. His recovery was slow and the temporary arrangement became permanent in 2008. Fidel outlasted nine American presidents, despite a fabled list of CIA assassination attempts.

## Fidel's Cuba

Castro's fledgling government immediately ordered
rents reduced, new wage
levels set, and estates limited
in size to 390 hectares (966
acres). A nationalisation programme followed, and the
government expropriated
factories, utilities and more
land, including an estimated
$8 billion of US assets. The
foundations were set for near-
universal state employment.
At the same time, the government instituted programmes

Castro by Guayasamin

to eradicate illiteracy and provide free universal schooling and
health care.

However, a centralised, all-powerful state didn't please all
Cubans. The media were soon placed under state control,
promised elections were never held, and Committees for the
Defence of the Revolution (CDRs) were established to keep
tabs on dissenters. In the early years of the Revolution, tens of
thousands of people suspected of being unsympathetic to its
goals were detained, imprisoned or sent to labor camps, along
with such other 'undesirables' as homosexuals and priests.

Between 1959 and 1962 about 200,000 Cubans, primarily professionals and affluent landowners, fled the country.
Expatriate Cubans settled in nearby Florida, establishing a colony that would steadily gain in political and economic power.
Another 200,000 abandoned Cuba as part of the Freedom
Flights Program between 1965 and 1971 and some 125,000
followed in 1980 when Castro lifted travel restrictions from
the port of Mariel.

Tank display at the Bay of Pigs

The US remained fundamentally opposed to Cuba's political evolution and sought to isolate Castro in Latin America. In 1961 CIA-trained Cuban exiles attempted to overthrow Castro's regime, resulting in the Bay of Pigs fiasco. Soon after, Castro declared himself a Marxist-Leninist. Castro had not displayed any Communist inclinations in the 1950s, and some suggest that US aggression pushed him to ingratiate himself with the powerful Soviet Union and its Eastern bloc of trading partners.

In 1962 Soviet President Nikita Khrushchev installed 42 medium-range nuclear missiles in Cuba. US President John F. Kennedy imposed a naval blockade on the island to ensure no more missiles arrived and insisted that the existing ones be removed. After six days of eyeball-to-eyeball challenge (known as the 'Cuban Missile Crisis'), Khrushchev backed down in return for the withdrawal of US nuclear missiles from Turkey. The same year saw the imposition of a trade embargo by the US (which Cubans call the *bloqueo*), and which remains in force to this day.

## The Special Period

Until the end of the 1980s, Soviet trade and subsidies were crucial factors in propping up Cuba's heavily centralised and often badly planned economy. But the subsequent dismantling of the Soviet Union left Cuba bereft of food, oil and hard currency. The government announced the start of a 'Special Period' in 1990, introducing new austerity measures. Though rationing had existed since 1962, it was increased to cover many more basic items. To make matters worse, in 1992 the Cuba Democracy Act extended the US embargo to cover a ban on trade with Cuba for foreign subsidiaries of US companies.

With its economy in disarray, the government introduced a limited number of capitalist measures while maintaining a firm political grip. Foreign investment, in the form of joint ventures in the fields of tourism and mineral and oil exploration, was keenly encouraged.

Further measures, such as the legalisation of small enterprises in 1993 and the introduction of farmers' markets in 1994, improved the welfare of some Cubans. Life was still hard, however, and in August 1994 30,000 Cubans fled to Florida on makeshift rafts. Today, the harshest days of privation have receded and a legal migration quota of 20,000 people a year is accepted into the US.

## A New Era
Castro turned 80 in 2006, but had to hand power temporarily to his brother, Raúl, while he underwent surgery. After making

## The Bay of Pigs Invasion

On 17 April 1961, a force of 1,297 Cuban exiles landed at Playa Girón. The Cubans were CIA-trained and came from US ships waiting offshore; US-piloted planes had bombed Cuban airfields days before. President Kennedy was unwilling to commit US troops on the ground or order further air strikes (US participation was denied at every stage). Castro's 20,000 troops, assisted by artillery and tanks, repelled the invasion within 65 hours. Some 1,180 exiles were captured and ransomed for US$53 million worth of food and medicine. The victory greatly boosted Castro's domestic and international status. Soon after, he declared Cuba a socialist, one-party state.

a slow recovery, he was not strong enough to take up the reins of government again. In 2008 Raúl was chosen as president of the Council of State and the Council of Ministers.

Raúl Castro's first measures were to lift a range of restrictions on consumer spending for those with access to foreign currency. Cubans may now own mobile phones and DVD players, rent cars and stay in tourist hotels on the beach. Some criminals had their death sentences commuted and two UN human rights treaties were signed after long being opposed by Fidel.

Putting public finances in order is a high priority. Agriculture has been decentralised and farmers given greater autonomy as part of a drive for greater production and efficiency. The number of state employees is being drastically cut, while permitted categories of self employment have been widened. The number of items in the ration book has been cut with the aim of eliminating the ration system entirely.

The leadership has been reorganised and corruption penalised. Men who were assumed to be successors to Fidel have been sidelined or charged with corruption offences and replaced by military colleagues of Raúl. It is still far from clear who will eventually take over from the Castros.

The ubiquitous image of Che

The end of 2014 saw a thaw in US-Cuba relations as President Barack Obama announced its will to restore normal diplomatic relations and lift the economic embargo. The negotiations between two countries began in earnest at the beginning of 2015.

# Historical Landmarks

**1492** Christopher Columbus lands in eastern Cuba.

**1511** Diego Velázquez begins Spanish settlement.

**1519** Havana, founded in 1515, moved to its present site.

**1868–78** Ten Years' War for Cuban independence - victory for Spanish forces.

**1886** End of slavery in Cuba.

**1895** War of Independence begins; José Martí killed.

**1898** Sinking of the USS *Maine*; US defeats Spain, which surrenders Cuba to the US.

**1902** Formation of the Republic of Cuba.

**1933–58** Fulgencio Batista holds power as president.

**1953** Fidel Castro launches failed attack on the Moncada Barracks.

**1956–9** Cuban Revolution. Castro seizes power (1 January 1959).

**1960** Castro's government nationalises all US businesses in Cuba without compensation.

**1961** CIA-trained Cuban exiles defeated at the Bay of Pigs.

**1962** Cuban Missile Crisis.

**1990** Russian trade and subsidies disappear; new austerity measures begin.

**1993** Economic reforms begin, including acceptance of foreign investment and self-employment.

**1994** Exodus of some 30,000 rafters to Florida; most are returned to Guantánamo Bay Naval Base.

**2003** Worldwide criticism of Cuba's human rights record after imprisonment of 78 dissidents and execution of three hijackers.

**2006** Fidel Castro temporarily hands power to his brother Raúl due to abdominal surgery.

**2008** Fidel Castro announces that he will not stand for president; Raúl Castro is elected president.

**2014** US President Barack Obama announces he wants to normalise diplomatic relations with Cuba and lift the economic embargo.

**2015** American-Cuban negotiations on restoring normal diplomatic relations begin.

# WHERE TO GO

To the surprise of many first-time visitors, Cuba is no speck in the Caribbean. Nicolás Guillén, the nation's finest poet, described the island as a 'long green alligator'. Long it certainly is, at 1,250km (776 miles) from snout to tail. Nearly the size of England in terms of area, Cuba is divided into 14 provinces and incorporates some 450 offshore islands, known as cayos ('cays' or 'keys').

Given its size, you would need at least a month to explore Cuba fully. Most people begin their journeys in the capital, Havana, before heading to the prized tobacco lands further west and doubling back across the plains of sugar cane and some of the country's finest colonial towns in central Cuba. The eastern region, known as Oriente, has soaring mountains and Cuba's second and most vibrant musical city, Santiago de Cuba.

Resort hotels hug quintessential Caribbean beaches (mostly to the north) and although many package tourists stick to the coast, every region has charming, engaging towns, beguiling visitors to explore further.

## HAVANA (LA HABANA)

The island's capital, **Havana ❶ (La Habana)**, with little over 2 million inhabitants, is one of the most intoxicating cities in the world. Ever since its early maritime days and through the 1950s – when gangsters who ran prostitution and gambling rackets made Havana synonymous with decadence – it has always held a slightly seedy, languorous allure. That nostalgic appeal is still evident.

A street in Santiago de Cuba

Colonial buildings in Old Havana

Today Havana is a one-of-a-kind, fascinating study in decay and rebirth. Unrestrained ocean waves and salty sea spray have eroded elegant buildings and the seawall of the Malecón, the sumptuous promenade and roadway that traces the edge of the sea. Throughout the city, crumbling houses three and four storeys tall, somehow still standing, line backstreets where children play stickball and adults survey the street from their balconies or doorways. In Old Havana, magnificently restored colonial palaces and stately Baroque churches and convents crowd pulsating squares. Once the finest colonial city in the Americas, Havana's grandeur has not been destroyed even by decades of crisis and neglect. No less defiant than Fidel Castro himself, beneath the rubble this city is a living, breathing, vital and sensual creature.

Havana sprawls over more than 700 sq km (270 sq miles) and is divided into many districts. Those of greatest interest are Habana Vieja (Old Havana), Centro Habana (Central

Havana), Vedado and – to a lesser extent – Miramar. The latter two districts are 20th century residential and shopping barrios that extend west and south of the old city. While most areas within a neighbourhood can be covered comfortably on foot, passing from one to the other usually requires a taxi or *cocotaxi* (a buggy powered by a motorcycle engine).

## Old Havana (La Habana Vieja)

The oldest section of Havana is the city's most spectacular, even if restoration work and gleaming coats of pastel colonial colours are leaving parts of it with a slightly more sanitised feel than the weathered working class neighbourhoods that extend along the water and inland. As the location of the city's greatest historical sites, **Old Havana** is where you'll want to spend most of your time.

First founded in 1515 on the south coast, Havana was moved to this site along a vast natural harbour in 1519. During the 16th century a fleet of galleons laden with treasures used the port as a pit stop on the way back to Spain from the New World. By the late 16th century, pirate attacks prompted the building of extensive city defences – colossal forts, a chain across the harbour mouth, and prominent city walls – making Havana the 'Bulwark of the West Indies'.

The wealthiest residents lived with their slaves in grand mansions constructed in the *mudéjar* style, a Christian-Muslim architectural tradition dating from the Spanish medieval period. Cool courtyards bathed in penumbral light sheltered from the sun and street noise behind massive doors, slatted blinds, carved iron window bars (*rejas*) and half-moon stained-glass windows (*mediopuntos*).

### Find that street

Cuban addresses usually include the street followed by a number. Helpful hints are also given: 'e/ …' ('between the streets …') or 'esq. …' ('corner of …').

Getting around in Havana

The presence of such architectural wonders, no matter how dilapidated, led Unesco to add Old Havana (along with the city's early fortifications) to its World Heritage List in 1982. In the central tourist quarter buildings have been or are being spruced up, mainly with funds raised by the City Historian's Office, headed by Eusebio Leal Spengler. Once restored, the buildings are turned into hotels, museums and galleries, or become once more the splendid old shops they used to be. Many other buildings are propped up by wooden columns: their arcades, fluted pillars and mosaic tiles teetering on their last legs, awaiting their turn. At night, away from the main restaurant and bar areas, the darkness of the streets is punctuated only by the neon glow of television sets from tiny front rooms and the occasional headlights of gas-guzzling vintage Chevrolets and Plymouths, though much of the historical centre is now a pedestrians-only zone.

Havana's past lives on, evoked in part by legendary locations from the pages of popular novels and the lives of fiction writers. These include Graham Greene's **Hotel Sevilla**, where 'Our Man in Havana' went to meet his secret service contact, and Ernest Hemingway's favourite watering holes (El Floridita and La Bodeguita del Medio), as well as the **Hotel Ambos Mundos**, where he penned much of *For Whom the Bell Tolls*.

Old Havana is best experienced on foot, although you can also pick up a *bicitaxi* for a tour around the district with stops for photos.

*Plaza de la Catedral*

Havana's sumptuous **Plaza de la Catedral** , the focus of Habana Vieja life, could be a stage set. Tourists linger at El Patio's outdoor café, sipping coffee or mojitos and tapping their toes to Cuban *son*. The all-hours hubbub here is infectious. The glorious Baroque facade and asymmetrical belltowers of the late 18th-century **cathedral** are the square's top attraction. The church, begun by Jesuits in 1748, is a thing of beauty; one half expects its bells to erupt in triumphant song. Its interior is surprisingly plain, but it once held the remains of Christopher Columbus. Just south of the cathedral are superb colonial mansions with bright shutters and *mediopuntos*, and an attractive little cul-de-sac **(Callejón de Chorro)** with a graphic arts workshop.

Of particular interest in the Cathedral Square is the **Museo de Arte Colonial** (San Ignacio 61 e/ Empedrado y O'Reilly; daily

The cathedral with its Baroque facade

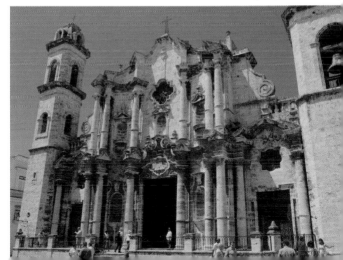

> ### A writer's tipples
>
> 'My mojitos at La Bodeguita, my daiquiris at El Floridita'– a personal declaration of drinks and where to have them, attributed to novelist Ernest Hemingway.

9.30am–6.30pm; www.habana cultural.ohc.cu) housed in a handsome palace dating from 1622. Its most important occupant, Lieutenant Colonel Don Luís Chacón lived there from 1726. Its little-altered architectural features are complemented by a large collection of 17th- and 18th-century furniture and 18th- and 19th-century tableware, as well as a wonderful collection of historic fans.

Just round the corner, you'll find the atmospheric bar-restaurant **La Bodeguita del Medio** ❸ (Empedrado 207 e/ Cuba y San Ignacio; restaurant: noon–midnight, bar: 9am–midnight), which according to Hemingway served Havana's finest mojito. Like pilgrims to Ernest's drinking shrine, all tourists seem required to pay their respects here and pay for an overpriced mojito. Art exhibitions are held down the street at the **Centro de Arte Contemporáneo Wifredo Lam** (San Ignacio, 22 esq. Empedrado; Mon–Sat 10am–5pm; free; www.wlam.cult.cu), named after Cuba's most famous 20th-century artist. Books, manuscripts and photographs of the country's best-known novelist are housed inside the **Fundación Alejo Carpentier** (Empedrado, 215 e/ Cuba y San Ignacio; Mon–Fri 8.30am–4.30pm; www.fundacioncarpentier.cult.cu; free).

## Plaza de Armas

**Plaza de Armas** ❸, which surrounds a statue of the patriot Céspedes and is ringed by shaded marble benches and second-hand bookstalls, is Havana's oldest square. It dates to the city's founding in 1519.

On the square's eastern side a small neoclassical temple, **El Templete**, marks the spot where the first Catholic mass was celebrated in 1519. Next door is one of the city's most luxurious hotels, Hotel Santa Isabel. To the north, the squat but angular and moated **Castillo de la Real Fuerza** (Fort of the Royal Forces; Tue–Sun 9.30am–5pm) is one of the oldest forts in the Americas, begun in 1558.

The battlements afford views over the harbour, and the bronze *La Giraldilla* weather vane on one of the fort's towers – depicting a woman scanning the seas for her lost husband, an early Cuban governor – has been adopted as the symbol of the city and of Havana Club rum.

In 1791 the seat of government and the governor's (or captain general's) residence were transferred from the fort to the newly built, Baroque **Palacio de los Capitanes Generales** on the square's western flank. A magnificent structure that was the presidential palace and then the municipal palace until Castro seized power, it now houses the **Museo de la Ciudad de la Habana** (Museum of the City of Havana; Tue–Sun 9.30am–5pm; English-speaking guides). Beyond the courtyard with a statue of Columbus lies a succession of splendid marbled and chandeliered rooms, some housing old cannon-balls and coaches, others decked out with gilded furnishings. The most hallowed room commemorates Cuba's 19th-century independence wars, with the first

Statue on Plaza de Armas

Shopping in Calle Obispo

Cuban flag and venerated personal objects from generals of the day.

### Calle Obispo

Running from Plaza de Armas to Parque Central, the pedestrianised **Calle Obispo D** is Old Havana's most important thoroughfare. Here you will find some smart shops catering to those with CUCs to spend, and you can peer into the courtyards of Havana's oldest homes. Equally fascinating are the two parallel, partly residential streets – O'Reilly and Obrapía – where neoclassical and colonial buildings intermingle with decrepit tenements. Restored Old Havana now extends all the way to Plaza Vieja and along pretty much all of Calle Obispo.

At no. 155, Museo de la **Farmacia Taquechel** (e/ Mercaderes y San Ignacio; daily 9am–5pm) is a beautifully restored pharmacy dating back to 1896, with floor-to-ceiling mahogany shelves supporting a lovely collection of 19th century porcelain jars containing herbal remedies and potions.

Close by, on the corner of Mercaderes and Obispo, is the refurbished 1920s-era **Hotel Ambos Mundos**; Hemingway lived on and off in room 511 for a couple of years during the 1930s. The room is kept as it was during his time here. Those not staying in the hotel can visit the room for a small fee, or go to the rooftop bar for cocktails and see the views over Old Havana.

Nearby are several museums worth visiting as much for the glorious colonial mansions that house them as for their

contents. The striking lemon-yellow **Casa de la Obra Pía**
(Calle Obrapía, 158 e/ Mercaderes and San Ignacio; Tue–
Sat 9am–5pm, until 12.30pm on Sun; www.habanacultural.
ohc.cu) is a 17th-century architectural wonder featuring a
magnificent portal brought from Cadiz in 1686. There is a
lovely courtyard and the rooms have been adapted as exhibition space for art and textiles. The owner, a member of one
of Cuba's most important families, sponsored five orphan
girls each year – an *obra pía* (work of piety) that lends its
name to both the house and its street. The massive mansion
opposite, nearly as impressive, houses the **Casa de África**
(Obrapía 157; Tue–Sat 9.30am–5pm, Sun 9.30am–1pm;

## Santería: The Cult of the Gods

*Santería* ('saint worship') is a syncretic religion derived from the Yoruba
people in Nigeria and developed in Cuba by African slaves. Practitioners
worship a complex pantheon of deities *(orishas)*, each with a specific
character and a parallel Catholic saint – a guise that allowed slaves to
disguise the religion from their hostile owners.

Initiates are chosen by a particular *orisha*, and they will wear the specific coloured beads of that saint and maintain shrines in their homes.
The saints are believed to exercise control over almost every aspect of a
person's life, but to communicate with them on matters of great impor-
tance, believers need the assistance of a *babalao* (priest), who will throw
shells and perform other rituals to learn of the saints' commands. Saints'
days are celebrations featuring Afro-Cuban drumming and dancing.

Many Cubans have at one time practised the rituals of santería –
even Castro, allegedly. While difficult to quantify, its popularity appears
to be increasing. In many parts of Cuba, one can see people wearing the
coloured beads of their saint – red and white for Changó, the powerful
god of war, and blue and white for Yemayá, the goddess of the sea – and
others dressed all in white for initiation rights 'to become sainted'.

Classic cars line the streets

www.habanacultural.ohc.cu), with pelts, drums, costumes, carved figures and furniture from some 26 African countries, as well as a collection of objects related to *santería*, the syncretic Afro-Cuban religion (see page 33) and various items related to Cuban slavery, such as manacles and traps.

On Calle Oficios at no. 16 lies the **Casa de los Árabes** (e/ Obispo y Obrapía; Tue–Sat 8.30am–5pm, Sun 9am–1pm; free), a 17th-century Moorish-style building that displays carpets, robes and pottery, and contains Havana's only mosque (an ornate room upstairs). There's a lovely courtyard restaurant attached.

The streets of Havana are a living museum of chrome-finned wondercars imported during Detroit's heyday. Several that once belonged to pivotal Cuban figures – such as a 1918 Ford truck used by Fidel's father and Camilo Cienfuegos' Oldsmobile – are lined up in the **Museo del Automóvil ⓔ** (Calle Oficios, 13 e/ Justiz y Obrapía; Tue–Sun 9.30am–5pm, until 1pm on Sun).

Further south along Calle Oficios, is the splendidly restored **Plaza de San Francisco ⓕ**, with upmarket restaurants and the imposing 18th-century **Convento de San Francisco de Asís** (daily 9am–6pm). The convent contains a museum of religious treasures and a beautiful cloister. Concerts are frequently held here. Nearby, you'll find several impeccable colonial-era houses with brilliantly coloured façades.

*Plaza Vieja*

Follow Calle Mercaderes to the fascinating **Plaza Vieja**
(Old Square), which was originally conceived in 1587. It has
received a massive facelift, with assistance from Unesco, and
a neoclassical marble fountain gleams incongruously in the
centre. On the south side, a fine 18th-century palace, known
as **La Casona**, has been converted into an arts centre; its
balcony gives a lovely view of the plaza. On the southwestern corner is the **Cervecería Taberna de la Muralla**, an
organic microbrewery with café and bar, offering welcome
respite. In the northeastern corner, on the roof of a yellow-
and-white wedding cake of a building, is the **Cámara
Oscura** (daily 9am–6pm), which gives up-close views of the
city as well as wider vistas. The old backstreets here are full
of character. Down Calle Cuba, between Sol and Luz, stands
the renovated 17th-century **Convento de Santa Clara**

Plaza Vieja has been meticulously restored

The Capitolio Nacional

(Mon–Fri 8.30am–5pm). A convent until 1919, it is now an architectural conservation centre.

By the railway station, between Calles Picota and Egido, is **Casa Natal de José Martí** (at Calle Leonor Pérez, 314; Tue–Sat 9.30am–5pm, Sun until 1pm), the modest birthplace of poet and statesman José Martí. The numerous personal effects on display here leave no doubt about the fact that Martí is Cuba's pre-eminent national hero.

*Capitolio*

Calle Brasil (also called Teniente Rey) leads directly west from Plaza Vieja to the monumental **Capitolio** **H** (Mon–Fri 9am–8pm, a replica of the American capitol in Washington, DC. Completed in 1929, it reflects the period when Cuba was in the thrall of the United States. Its vast bronze doors pictorially chart the island's history, and the immense main gallery inside has a replica diamond in the floor beneath the dome, that marks the spot from which all distances in the country are measured.

Directly behind the Capitolio is the **Fábrica de Tabacos Partagás** **I** (Partagás Cigar Factory; Industria, 520 e/ Dragones y Barcelona; Tue–Fri; 40-minute tours start every 15 mins, 9–11am and noon–1.30pm; no photos allowed), the biggest export factory in the country – with more than 200 rollers churning out 5 million cigars a year – and one of Havana's top tourist draws. This factory, which has been rolling out *puros* since the mid-19th century, is the best to visit on the island; it also has a fine tobacco shop (open Mon–Sat all day) and smoking lounge for aficionados. Bear in mind that customs regulations are tight: you're allowed to take home only 23 individual cigars without official receipt, and fakes (see page 95) are likely to be confiscated.

Just east of the Capitolio, on Parque Central near the classic Hotel Inglaterra, stands the magnificent **Gran Teatro de la Habana** ❿, completed in 1837. The home of the Cuban National Ballet and Opera drips with ornate balustrades, shutters and sculpted columns. The cavernous interior is hardly less awesome but can only be visited during performances.

Those with the Hemingway bug can visit **El Floridita** ⓚ (www.floridita-cuba.com), at the intersection of Calles Obispo and Montserrate, one block east of Parque Central. The writer immortalised the swanky bar in *Islands in the Stream*. A bronze statue of Papa now leans against the bar, his photos adorn the walls, and his favourite daiquiri is now referred to as the 'Papa Hemingway', with double rum and no sugar (barmen claim he was diabetic). At CUC$6 a daiquiri, the place is a bit of a tourist trap, but still capable of evoking the kind of hedonistic refuge expat writers adored.

On the same side of the Parque Central is the Art Deco **Museo Nacional de Bellas Artes** (www.bellasartes.cult.cu; Tue–Sat 9am–5pm, Sun 8am–2pm combined ticket available with

The Partagás Cigar Factory

the Arte Cubano collection). Many of the paintings were left behind by ruling-class families who fled Cuba in 1959. This building contains the **Arte Universal** **L** collection, while a few blocks northeast on Trocadero is the **Arte Cubano** **M** section, an excellent collection housed in the 1954 Fine Arts Palace.

Another few blocks northeast, housed in the grand presidential palace used by presidents (and dictators) between 1920 and 1959, is the **Museo de la Revolución** **N** (daily 10am–5pm; English-speaking guides), Cuba's largest and most fascinating museum. Allow a couple of hours to see this exhaustive exhibition of the trajectory of the 1959 Cuban Revolution. The most absorbing sections chart the struggle to power with countless maps, evocative photos of both torture victims and triumphal scenes, and assorted personal memorabilia from passports and worn-out shoes to Kalashnikov rifles and blood-stained clothes. In the square outside is the *Granma*, the boat that carried Castro and his 81 rebels from Mexico to Cuba in 1956; it is now enclosed in glass, guarded by military police and surrounded by other revolutionary relics, such as a tractor converted into a tank and the delivery van used in the failed attack on the Presidential Palace in 1957.

A building on the Prado

*The Prado*

West of the oldest sections and intimate streets of Old Havana is an area of wide boulevards and grand palaces. The loveliest avenue, the **Paseo del Prado** ⓪ (officially known as Paseo de Martí), runs from Parque Central to the sea and officially separates Old Havana from Centro. It was built in the 18th century as a promenade outside the old city walls. Grand but run-down buildings, with fading flamingo-pink and lime-green façades, and ornate columns, flank a raised promenade of laurels, gas lamps and marble benches. In the 19th century, after the city walls collapsed, this was the most fashionable

Swimming off the rocks at the Malecón

strolling ground for the city's wealthy. Now it serves as a mini-park for *habaneros*, from musicians and roaming couples to children playing on homemade skateboards and go-karts, or practising baseball shots.

## Havana's Forts

Cuba's most impressive forts sit brooding over the capital's commercial harbour. Take a taxi through the road tunnel beneath the water to reach them. The older one, built at the end of the 16th century, is the **Castillo de los Tres Santos Reyes Magos del Morro ℗**, better known as 'El Morro' (daily 8am–10pm). The views of Havana over the defiant cannons are magical.

The vast **Fortaleza de San Carlos de la Cabaña ℚ**, known as 'La Cabaña' (daily 8am–11pm), running beside the harbour, was constructed after the English capture of Havana in 1763. The largest fort ever built in the Americas, it is well-preserved, and the gardens and ramparts are romantically lit in the evening. A ceremony held at 9pm (El Cañonazo) re-enacts the firing of a cannon that marked the closing of the city gates.

## New Havana

The walls surrounding Old Havana were razed during the 19th century to allow the city to expand westwards. The long, curvaceous and crumbling **Malecón** (breakwater), a six-lane highway and promenade alongside the city's north shore, links the districts of Centro and Vedado. The victim of harmful salt spray, the seafront drive is undergoing patchy renovation. Havana's youth congregate along the Malecón on fine evenings, flying kites, canoodling, swimming off the rocks, and setting out to sea in giant inner tubes to fish.

Although most visitors will want to concentrate on historic Old Havana, the newer districts provide a fascinating view of the areas where most people live and work. The most interesting districts of **New Havana** are Centro and Vedado. The former is a congested, lower-middle-class *barrio* (neighbourhood) with few attractions, although a walk along its dusty streets can be an eye-opening experience. Vedado is the city's principal commercial and residential zone – the epicentre of middle-class Havana – with parks, monuments, hotels, restaurants, theatres and the University of Havana. Once the stomping ground of the elite in the 1950s, the 'suburb' of Miramar today is home to foreign companies investing in Cuba and numerous diplomatic missions of foreign governments.

Eating out in Chinatown

## Centro

**Centro Habana** (Central Havana) is a ramshackle residential and commercial area. The city's main shopping street, **Calle San Rafael**, traverses it from the Parque Central westwards. This might be Havana at its least guarded. You can stop to have your nails painted, or get a shave and a haircut, right there on the pavement. One of the private markets has overrun Havana's small **Chinatown**, at Calles Zanja and Rayo. A few Chinese restaurants selling Cuban-Oriental food are all that remain of what was once the largest Chinatown in Latin America in the 1950s.

The neighbourhood of **Cayo Hueso**, just behind the Malecón, is a rough-and-tumble barrio once populated by cigar-factory workers. Today the main reason to visit is to see **Callejón Hamel ®**, where the artist Salvador González has dedicated himself to preserving the area's Afro-Cuban culture. González's studio is here, and on Sunday at noon–3pm there are performances of Afro-Cuban ritual and rumba.

## Vedado

**Vedado** is a respectable business district as well as a leafy residential area, spacious and orderly in comparison with Habana Vieja and Centro. It had its heyday in the 1940s and 1950s, when such gangsters as Meyer Lansky held sway in the Nacional, Riviera and Capri hotels. Stars like Frank Sinatra and Ginger Rogers performed, and American tourists emptied their wallets in glittering casinos.

The Revolution put the lid on the nightlife by banning gambling and deporting the Mafiosi. Today, new or refurbished hotels of international standard welcome travellers on business or for pleasure.

Business is centred on **La Rampa**, the name for Calle 23 from Calle L to the sea. Opposite the tower-block Hotel Habana Libre – the Havana Hilton in pre-revolutionary days – is the **Coppelia**

**Ice Cream Park** $. At this institution, locals queue for hours for the prized ice cream, ladling them into saucepans to take home. Foreigners can join the queue as well; payment is in *moneda nacional*. Coppelia was instrumental in the award-winning Cuban film *Fresa y Chocolate* ('Strawberry and Chocolate'), a daring film when it came out in 1994 which dealt with freedoms, homosexuality and revolutionary fervour in contemporary Havana (its title is a wry reference to the lack of choices of ice cream flavours — indeed, of all things — in Cuba).

Coppelia ice cream seller

A short walk up the hill brings you to the University of Havana, founded in the early 18th century, a quiet, attractive campus of neo-classical buildings.

Directly east on Calle San Miguel, 1159 between Calles Ronda and Mazón is the **Museo Napoleónico** (Mon–Sat 10am–6pm). The mansion holds not only Empire furniture but also a remarkable collection of Napoleonic memorabilia: portraits, busts and even his pistol, hat and a cast of his death mask from St Helena. The house and contents were appropriated by the state from a rich owner in 1960.

In the same year, the government acquired the **Museo de Artes Decorativas** (Calle 17, 502 e/ D y E; Tue–Sat 10.30am–6.30pm, Sun 10am–12.30pm), when its aristocratic owner fled the island, leaving her collection of fine art hidden in

The iron sculpture of Che on Plaza de la Revolución

the basement. Each room in this grand 19th-century villa is furnished in a particular style: English Chippendale, Chinese, Baroque or Art Deco.

Massive marble mausoleums line the principal avenues of the **Cementerio de Cristóbal Colón** 🅣 (Columbus Cemetery; entrance on Zapata y 12; daily 7am–5pm), which is a vast city of the dead established in the late 19th century. Cubans come here to pray and place flowers at the tomb of La Milagrosa ('The Miracle Worker'), who helps people in need. It is said that she was buried with her infant at her feet, but when their bodies were exhumed, the child was cradled in her arms.

## Plaza de la Revolución

The **Plaza de la Revolución** 🅤 is a vast, stark concourse where political rallies are held; otherwise it is usually empty. The square is dominated by grim high-rise ministry buildings, erected in the 1950s by Batista, and the **José Martí Memorial** – a giant, tapering obelisk that looks like a rocket launch pad – with a pensive marble statue of Cuba's greatest hero and a **museum** about his life (Mon–Sat 9.30am–5.30pm). The obelisk's lookout gives superb panoramic views. Adorning the Ministry of the Interior building opposite is a giant iron sculpture-mural of Che, illuminated at night. South of Plaza de Revolucion at Calle 26, esq. Calle 11, is **Fábrica de Arte Cubano** (Thu–Sun 8pm–4am, Sun until 2am; www.fabricadeartecubano.com), a popular venue for concerts, art exhibitions, film screenings and much more that attracts trendy crowds of habaneros as well as savvy tourists.

## Miramar

To the west is the exclusive district of **Miramar**. The villas of the pre-revolutionary rich, expropriated by the state, have now been turned into apartments or offices, but embassies along Avenida 5 still imbue the area with a privileged feel.

At the corner of Calle 14, the **Museo del Ministerio del Interior** (Tue–Fri 9am–5pm Sat 9am–4pm) has some intriguing exhibits relating to CIA espionage, including code boxes concealed in briefcases, decoding equipment, a transmitter hidden in a fake rock, and a range of explosive devices. It also documents dozens of the CIA's attempts to assassinate Fidel Castro. Don't miss the Russian Embassy, between Calles 62 and 66, which looks like a giant concrete robot.

Growing as an attraction, the 22m long and 8m wide **Maqueta de la Habana** (Calle 28, 113 e/ Avenida 1 y 3; Tue–Sat 9.30am–5pm) is an intricate scale model of the city in astounding 1:1,000 detail. A visit to the Maqueta can help organise the city's neighbourhoods in your mind.

Also worth a visit is beautifully restored Casa de las Tejas Verdes (Green Roof Tiles House; Calle 2 no. 318 esq. 5ta Avenida; Mon–Fri 9am–5pm) dating from 1926

## Casa de la Música

The Casa de la Música in Miramar is one of the best shows in town. This is where Cubans come to dance their hearts out to salsa and other rhythms played by live bands. And foreigners join in too.

and now housing a centre for promoting modern architecture and design. It organises interesting expositions, workshops and offers guided tours.

## Ernie and Graham: Literary Footprints

Ernest Hemingway's literary and personal footprints are as deep in Cuba as they are in Spain, and they've become part of the tourist fabric in both places. Hemingway wrote two books based in Cuba, *The Old Man and The Sea* and *Islands in the Stream*, and in large part he wrote *For Whom the Bell Tolls* (about the Spanish Civil War) from his hotel room in Havana. He was an island resident for two decades. Pilgrims can trace his life in Cuba at various sights, including Finca La Vigía, Cojímar, El Floridita, La Bodeguita del Medio and the Hotel Ambos Mundos. Despite chummy photos with Castro (they met at the annual Hemingway Fishing Tournament, which Fidel won), the writer's views on the Revolution are elusive, although all Cubans accept him as a fervent supporter. His views notwithstanding, it is certain that he identified with the Cuban people. Hemingway abandoned Cuba in 1960 and committed suicide shortly thereafter in Idaho.

Graham Greene's classic novel about Cuban intrigue, *Our Man in Havana*, was first published in 1958. Not only is it an evocative portrait of sleazy 1950s Havana, with scenes set in the Nacional and Sevilla hotels and the Tropicana nightclub, it's also eerily prescient, as the hero invents drawings of Soviet weapons hidden in the Cuban countryside, long before Castro aligned the country with the USSR. Greene was a great supporter of the Revolution, praising Castro, the war against illiteracy, the lack of racial segregation, and the support of the arts. When he went to Cuba to do research for the book in 1958, he took supplies for Castro, who was secluded in the Sierra Maestra, in exchange for an interview that never took place. Greene's support wavered though when he learned of the Revolution's forced labour camps in the 1960s.

## Havana's Outskirts

Havana's sprawling suburbs contain a couple of places associated with Ernest Hemingway that are magnets for those seeking to trace the author's life in Cuba. From 1939 to 1960 he lived on and off in the **Finca Vigía**, now the **Casa Museo de Ernest Hemingway** (Wed–Mon 9am–5pm, Sun until 12.30pm; closed when it rains). The house is 11km (7 miles) southeast of Havana in San Francisco de Paula, so

A bust of Ernest Hemingway

you will have to take a taxi. Visitors may not enter the graceful villa, but by peering through windows you can see all the rooms furnished as the writer originally had them, covered in bullfighting posters and filled with more than 9,000 books, including such titles as *The Guide to Hunting and Fishing in Cuba*. You can roam the lush gardens searching out his motorboat, the *Pilar*, and the swimming pool where Ava Gardner once skinny-dipped.

Hemingway kept the *Pilar* 10km (6 miles) east of Havana at **Cojímar**. Next to the little fort is a Hemingway bust, looking out over the bay. His captain and cook aboard the *Pilar* was the fisherman Gregorio Fuentes. Until his death at the age of 104 in 2002, Gregorio would regale visitors with tales of his hero. He always denied that he was Santiago, the title character in *The Old Man and the Sea*, but he did not dispute that it was in Cojímar that Hemingway found the inspiration for his famous novel. The little fishing village is now a concrete jungle and unrecognisable from Hemingway's description.

Approximately 18km (11 miles) east of Havana (20 minutes' drive), the long, sandy **Playas del Este** (Eastern Beaches) are a big draw for Cubans. They are the closest beaches to the capital and particularly lively on Sundays.

## PINAR DEL RÍO PROVINCE

Due west of Havana is **Pinar del Río province**, Cuba's westernmost region – a finger of land with the Gulf of Mexico to the north and the Caribbean to the south. It contains some of Cuba's most beautiful countryside among the lush Guaniguanico mountains and surrounding patchwork of verdant fields, where the world's finest tobacco is cultivated. In the beautiful Viñales Valley, tobacco fields (*vegas*) and ancient limestone formations (*mogotes*) produce spectacular scenery more reminiscent of Southeast Asia than the Caribbean. In this resolutely agricultural region, oxen pulling ploughs that till the red-earth fields and cowboy farmers (*guajiros*) on horseback are much more common than cars. Residents of Havana might think of it as a poor backwater, but the easy, almost somnolent pace and breathtaking countryside make it one of Cuba's certain highlights.

There are beaches and excellent diving further west, but for most visitors the star attractions are the irresistible little town of Viñales and its beautiful valley. Many visitors take organised daytrips to the region from Havana hotels, but an overnight stay in Viñales – overlooking the valley – is highly recommended.

Start your explorations by driving west on the *autopista* (highway) linking Havana with the province's capital city of Pinar del Río. About 63km (39 miles) along the highway, a turnoff leaves the level, palm-dotted plains for **Soroa** ❷, where a richly endowed botanical garden nestles in the mountain foothills near a tourist complex. A guided tour reveals an orchid garden, lychee and mango trees, coffee plants and splendid specimens of *jagüey* and *ceiba* trees. There is a *mirador* (lookout) and a waterfall, while the restaurant in the Villa Soroa-Castillo de las Nubes complex also has stunning views over the mountains.

## Pinar del Río

At the end of the highway, 175km (109 miles) west of Havana, the small city of **Pinar del Río ❸** is a busy commercial centre. Along the main street, Calle José Martí, low-rise neoclassical buildings in blues, yellows, greens and orange have a stately but dilapidated quality. You'll find a small, touristy tobacco factory, **Fábrica de Tabacos Francisco Donatien** (Maceo 157; Mon–Fri 7am–5pm, Sat 8am–noon; no photos allowed), housed in an old jail near the Plaza de la Independencia. Visitors are welcome here and at the less picturesque **Fábrica de Bebidas Casa Garay** (Isabel Rubio 189; Mon–Fri

Oxen ploughing the Viñales Valley

7am–5pm, Sat 8am–noon), where they make a local sugar cane and wild guava liqueur called *guayabita del Pinar*.

The road southwest from the city to San Juan y Martínez leads deep into tobacco's heartland – the **Vuelta Abajo** – where the world's greatest tobacco is grown. Amid fields of big green leaves ripening in the sun and plantations covered in white gauze sheets stand steep-roofed barns where leaves are hung on poles with a needle and thread and then dried, turning them from green to brown.

If you continue to the western tip of the island you come to the **Península de Guanahacabibes ❹**, a Natural Biosphere Reserve covering 1,175 sq km (730 sq miles). At La Bajada the road divides, heading west 52km (32 miles) to **Cabo de San Antonio**, where there is a small hotel and marina. Alternatively, 12km (7 miles) south of La Bajada at **María la Gorda**, on the eastern shore of the **Bahía de Corrientes**, there is a hotel offering some of the best diving in Cuba.

Some 27km (17 miles) to the north of Pinar del Río lies the most picturesque corner of Cuba. The deeply green **Viñales Valley** is spattered with *mogotes*, sheer-sided limestone masses covered in thick vegetation. These are the remnants of a collapsed cavern system that was created underwater at least 150 million years ago, in the Jurassic period. Tobacco (of slightly lesser quality than in the Vuelta Abajo) grows here in a patchwork of fields and dries in *bohíos*, constructed with shaggy thatch. Cigar-chomping *guajiros* in huge straw hats urge on their oxen, as vultures swoop overhead. At any time of day you can wander the fields and meet the farmers, who might even offer you a cigar.

## Viñales

The little town of **Viñales ❺** is surprisingly spruce, with a fetching, arcaded main street and lovely rustic scenes along the back lanes. The best valley views can be had from either of its lovely hotels: Horizontes Los Jazmines and Horizontes La Ermita (see page 135). The sight at dusk is especially alluring.

Near the Cupet petrol station as you leave town heading north towards Puerto de Esperanza, is the delightful **Jardín Botánico**. The garden was first planted in the 1930s and has been maintained by the same family ever since. A guide will show you around the fruit trees and flowers and let you taste the produce (tip expected).

Nearby a couple of local tourist sights, on all the package excursions, have curiosity value but not much else. One limestone *mogote* just west of town was painted by local artists dangling on ropes in the 1960s with a **Mural de la Prehistoria** (Mural of Prehistory) – com-missioned by Castro himself – that is 120m (370ft) high and 180m (550ft) long. The garish painting, an exercise in bad judgment and sloppy execution, depicts evolution from an ammonite to a dinosaur to advanced (and presumably socialist) *Homo sapiens*. All the creatures depicted were indigenous to the area. Eight kilometres (5 miles) to the north of town, the extensive **Cueva del Indio** (Indian Cave) was used as a hideout by Indians after the conquest. A tour through the cave includes a brief ride on an underground river in a boat (which would-be emigrants once stole for an

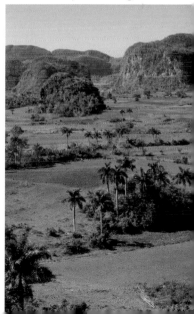

Viñales Valley and its mogotes

unsuccessful escape attempt to Florida). Both mural and cave have tourist restaurants.

## Islands North & South

Just off the province's north and south coasts are three contrasting islands. To the north, **Cayo Levisa** ❻ is a small coral cay, about 3km (2 miles) long and just several hundred metres wide at most points, which has pristine beaches, clear waters and coral reefs. The island is a half-hour ferry ride from Palma Rubia (ferries leave at 10.30am and 5.30pm). There's a well-equipped diving centre, and overnight accommodation is available in the simple Villa Cayo Levisa bungalow complex, which has a restaurant and a bar.

On the other side of Cuba, stretching eastwards from Pinar del Río's southern coast, is the Archipiélago de los Canarreos. There are two main islands. **Cayo Largo** ❼, 25km (16 miles) long and the most easterly of the archipelago, might be your Caribbean paradise – if all you're looking for is a dazzling white beach and clear blue seas. Other than the kilometres of beaches, there's not much else of consequence here except

Homo sapiens at the Mural de la Prehistoria

mangrove, scrub and half a dozen comfortable all-inclusive hotels with a full programme of entertainment and watersports. Turtles nest in the sand at one end of the island. At the other you can go sailing, diving and deep-sea fishing or take a boat trip to **Playa Sirena**, an incomparable strip of sand a 10-minute boat ride away, where lobster lunches are available.

Cayo Largo, with its captive tourist audience, is considerably more expensive than the mainland. Some package tourists spend the whole of their holiday on Cayo Largo. Those with low boredom thresholds might consider coming for the day or perhaps staying overnight, taking the half-hour flights from Havana and Varadero.

By contrast, the **Isla de la Juventud** ❽ (Isle of Youth) sees few tourists except those at the rather isolated Hotel El Colony (on the Siguanea Bay, half way along the island's western shore), who come exclusively for the superb diving off the island's south-

Inside Cueva del Indio

western tip. Cuba's largest offshore island, some 50km (31 miles) in diameter, the Isle of Youth is not its prettiest. It is said to have been the location for Robert Louis Stevenson's *Treasure Island*; pirates once buried their booty here. The island received its jaunty name in the 1970s, when as many as 22,000 foreign students (mainly from politically sympathetic African countries) studied here in no fewer than 60 schools.

The island fails to live up to its colourful past. The number of foreign students has dropped to fewer than 5,000, and derelict boarding schools dot the monotonous countryside. However, there are plenty of beaches to be discovered, and in a series of caves at **Punta del Este** you can examine enigmatic symbols painted centuries ago by Ciboney Indians (restricted access).

For more accessible entertainment, **Nueva Gerona**, the island's little capital, is moderately attractive, with striped awnings along its smart, pillared main street.

# MATANZAS PROVINCE

The province east of Havana – largely flat sugar-cane country – was in the 19th century Cuba's most important cane-producing region. For today's visitors, however, the focus is on the beach resort of Varadero, Cuba's biggest draw, with opportunities for side trips to atmospheric, time-warped towns and to the swamplands of the south coast.

## Varadero

**Varadero** ❾ has enthusiastic proponents and equally passionate detractors among its visitors. A long peninsula with many dozens of hotels and restaurants, bars, fast-food cafés and grocery shops stretching right to the tip (and more of each on the way), Varadero doesn't feel much like Cuba at all. It is a package tourist enclave, and plenty of visitors fly in and never venture further afield. If you want to see and learn what makes Cuba a fascinating place, though, you'll need to escape for at least a couple of daytrips. In towns around Cuba you'll meet tourists who – like jailbird escapees – rejoice at having got out of Varadero.

Still, there are plenty of delighted people for whom this is heaven: a 20km (12-mile) long, virtually uninterrupted white-sand beach

### Presidio Modelo

Just east of Nueva Gerona is the fascinating Presidio Modelo (Tue–Sat 9am–5pm, Sun 9am–1pm). The dictator Machado built this copy of a US penitentiary in 1931. Castro and 26 of his rebels were sent here after the storming of the Moncada Barracks; their ward and Castro's solitary confinement cell have been restored.

Souvenir sellers at Varadero

with shallow, clean waters. Varadero isn't a recent development by a government desperate for hard currency (though it may soon become a faceless cash cow not unlike Cancún). It was in the 1920s that Varadero first attracted millionaires, who built palatial holiday villas. They were led by Alfred Irenée Dupont who bought up most of the peninsula and used to vacation at the opulent **Mansion Xanadú**, which he had built in 1930 and which is now an exclusive six-room hotel, and club house of the 18-hole Xanadú golf course (www.varaderogolfclub. com). Tourism proper began after World War II with the construction of hotels and casinos.

However, the beach, Varadero's best feature, can be problematic. Northern winds kick up with considerable frequency, and lifeguards put out the red flags to warn of the dangerous undertow. There is often a strong smell from the oil pumps on the resort's outskirts. Prostitution and hassling are much less of a problem than they once were, but other pests (namely mosquitoes) can be a real annoyance. Moreover, the resort is spread out over 17km (11 miles), with no real centre, so you need transport to get around.

On the other hand, Varadero has many extremely comfortable hotels (most of them the results of international joint ventures), open bars and an excellent range of watersports. And, unlike other parts of Cuba, topless sunbathing is allowed here. If you tire of the beach, there are organised excursions to every conceivable point of interest on the island – including Havana.

Varadero occupies a long, thin insular spit of sand, with water on both sides and a bridge to the mainland. Between Calles 25 and 54 there's something of a local community of Cubans, with ancient Cadillacs parked outside rickety wooden bungalows. The liveliest area is around Calles 54 to 64, with a shopping mall, a host of restaurants and bars, and the **Retiro Josone**, a pretty park set around a palm-fringed boating lake. Spreading several kilometres further east are the newest hotel complexes.

## Matanzas and Cárdenas

These quintessentially Cuban provincial towns are a world apart from Varadero. Their poorly stocked shops, dusty backstreets and primitive transport provide Varadero's package tourists with a convenient insight into Cuban life before they're whisked back to their hotels.

**Matanzas ⑩**, 42km (26 miles) west of Varadero, is busy and grimy. Lying alongside a deep bay, it came into its own during the 19th century as the country's sugar capital. On the leafy main square, Parque Libertad, the **Museo Farmacéutico** (Mon–Fri 10am–6pm, Sun 8am–noon) is a wonderfully preserved chemist's shop, founded in 1882. On a street running east towards the bay, the neo-classical **Catedral de San Carlos Borromeo** is undergoing renovation.

A little further to the east, impressive buildings on Plaza de la Vigía include the **Palacio de Junco**, which houses

On the street at Cárdenas

a second-rate provincial museum, and the **Teatro Sauto**. Constructed in 1863, the lovely theatre has tiers of wrought-iron boxes and a painted ceiling.

**Las Cuevas de Bellamar** (daily 9am–5pm), a short distance east, are Cuba's oldest tourist attraction. The caves were discovered by chance in 1861 by a Chinese workman. Tours (in English) take you down into a vast chamber for views of the many stalactites and stalagmites.

Fortunes have changed for the town of **Cárdenas** ⓫, 15km (9 miles) east of Varadero. Once the island's most important sugar-exporting port, it's now a somewhat ramshackle place. But the main square is elegant, and the **Museo Municipal Oscar María de Rojas** (Plaza Echeverría e/ Avenidas 4 y 6; Tue–Sat 10am–6pm, Sun 9am–1pm), the second oldest museum in the country, houses a quirky collection of items. There is also the **Museo de la Batalla de Ideas** (Calle 12 y Plaza Eheverría; Tue–Sat 9am–6pm, Sun 9am–noon). Inaugurated by Castro in

2001, it documents the campaign for the repatriation of Elián, a local boy who was at the centre of international controversy in 1999–2000. His mother died while fleeing with him to Miami, but after months of heated controversy he was returned by the US authorities to live with his father.

## Zapata Peninsula

The **Zapata Peninsula** is the largest wetland area in the Caribbean, flat as a pancake and covered in mangrove swamps and grassland plains. Its protected wildlife includes crocodiles, manatees and numerous species of birds. Frankly, though, you are unlikely to see any interesting wildlife unless you take a guided bird-watching trip from **Playa Larga**. You can see penned reptiles at the crocodile farm at **La Boca**, a popular tourist site where you can pose with a baby croc and try crocodile steak.

Zapata Peninsula

A more appealing prospect is picturesque **Guamá** ⓬, a half-hour boat ride from La Boca along an artificial channel and then across the vast **Laguna del Tesoro** (Treasure Lake). Legend has it that the Indians dumped their

### Battle beach

'Playa Girón: La Primera Derrota del Imperialismo en América Latina' ('The First Defeat of Imperialism in Latin America') – billboard at Bay of Pigs.

jewels into the water rather than surrender them to Spanish *conquistadores*. Guamá is a group of tiny islands connected by wooden bridges. A few visitors stay in the thatched *cabañas*, but most just come to wander along the boardwalk, greet the ducks and egrets, and have a meal.

It may be peaceful now, but the Zapata Peninsula is best known for the violence and bloodshed that once visited its shores. South of La Boca you soon come to Playa Girón – site of the 1961 US-led **Bay of Pigs** invasion (see page 21), in which more than 100 people were killed. At irregular intervals along the often crab-infested road are a number of concrete memorials to those who died during the invasion. There are two simple, isolated bungalow hotel complexes on the bay, one at quiet **Playa Larga**, the other at **Playa Girón** ⓭, where the already scruffy beach is further spoiled by a concrete breakwater. One major attraction, however, is the excellent **Museo Playa Girón** (daily 9am–5pm) which serves as an emotional memorial to the three-day Bay of Pigs debacle.

## CENTRAL CUBA

Tourists usually whiz through central Cuba. The only tourist beacons are on or near the coasts: in the south around Cienfuegos and at Trinidad, and in the north at Cayo Coco and Guillermo and Playa Santa Lucía. But there is much else to see.

The Catedral de la Purísima Concepción, Cienfuegos

Central Cuba comprises five provinces: Cienfuegos, Villa Clara, Sancti Spíritus, Ciego de Avila and Camagüey. Each focuses on a provincial city of the same or similar name, typically of some interest yet not likely to detain you for longer than a day. The west has the best scenery, in the Sierra del Escambray mountains.

To the east of Sancti Spíritus, towns lie on flat plains. This used to be the main sugar cane growing area in the 1970s, but the collapse of the sugar-for-oil trade with the USSR in the 1990s led to the closure of many sugar factories. In Camagüey, the cattle-ranch province, watermills and *vaqueros* (cowboys) on horseback punctuate the skyline.

## Cienfuegos

The best feature of the port city of **Cienfuegos** ⓮ (250km/155 miles southeast of Havana) is its position, set at the back of a large bay. Despite the industry on its periphery, the centre is attractive, with pastel-coloured neoclassical buildings. Described as the 'Pearl of the South', it now has Unesco World Heritage Site status.

The focal point in town is **Parque José Martí**, one of the grandest squares in the country. Here you will find most of the major historical buildings, where the city was founded in 1819. The influence of 19th century French immigrants can be seen in the architecture, although there are several styles, including neoclassical and Art Deco. Take a guided tour of the town's finest colonial building, the **Teatro Tomás Terry**, on the north side of the square. Built in 1890, it was named after a rich sugar plantation owner, once a poor emigré from Venezuela. The interior, largely original, has a lovely frescoed ceiling and a semicircle of tiered boxes and wooden seats. Enrico Caruso and Sara Bernhardt once performed here, and on weekends you may be able to catch a performance by one of Cuba's top ballet companies. The **Catedral de la Purísima Concepción**, built in 1870, is on the east side of the square. It has an attractive interior with stained-glass windows depicting the 12 apostles.

The Paseo del Prado is the town's principal thoroughfare and the longest boulevard in Cuba, a palm-lined road that takes you down to the spit of land protruding into the bay past smart waterside villas. At the edge of Punta Gorda, near the end of the Malecón (Calle 37), is the spectacular **Palacio del Valle**. This kitsch, Moorish Revival-style mansion (with a few other styles mixed in),

## Botanical highlight

The Jardín Botánico Soledad (daily 8am–5pm), 23km (14 miles) outside Cienfuegos at Pepito Tey on the road to Trinidad, is the oldest botanical garden in Cuba (it dates from 1899) and one of the best tropical gardens in the world. Tour operators in Cienfuegos can arrange guided tours; alternatively, go straight there and join a tour at the entrance.

Trinidad's Plaza Mayor

was finished in 1917. It is now a restaurant with a rooftop bar and is attached to the Hotel Jagua alongside.

At the mouth of the bay, on the western side, the **Castillo de Jagua** (daily 9am–4pm) was constructed by the Spanish in 1733–45 (long before the city's founding in 1819) to ward off pirates. You reach the castle on a ferry from a terminal just south of the Parque Martí (Avenida 46 e/ Calles 23 y 25).

## Trinidad

The scenic, undulating 80km (50-mile) road east from Cienfuegos to Trinidad skirts the foothills of the Sierra del Escambray, Cuba's second-highest mountain range. The beguiling town of **Trinidad** ⑮, the third of Diego Velázquez's original seven settlements, subsequently became rich through the smuggling, slave and sugar trades. Its sizable old town is endowed with marvellous Spanish colonial architecture and has been named by Unesco as a World Heritage Site. Cuba could package it as a time capsule: it is the island's prettiest town and one of the finest preserved colonial cities in all the Americas. Even the cobblestone streets still remain in the old centre, which restrict traffic and make things difficult for bicycles and horses. There's been a preservation order on Trinidad since the 1950s.

Within easy striking distance of Trinidad are enough attractions to make a longer stay especially rewarding, including the fine beach of Playa Ancón, the lush Valle de los Ingenios (Valley of the Sugar Mills), and waterfalls and treks in the Escambray mountains.

Restored mansions of the well-to-do have been turned into museums, while art galleries, craft shops and restaurants occupy additional lovely old buildings. The city is known for its live music venues in the centre, several of which are open air or in covered courtyards of old buildings. However, entertainment is low key, and it's still a pleasant, relaxed place. If you spend a night here you can experience the town without the tour-bus hordes.

The old town clusters around the **Plaza Mayor**, a delightful square of painted railings, fanciful urns, greyhound statues and colonial buildings. The relatively plain church, Iglesia Parroquial de la Santísima Trinidad, is the largest in Cuba, with five aisles instead of three and hand-carved gothic altars. Beside it is the **Museo Romántico** (Tue–Sun 9am–5pm) with a collection of fine furniture and porcelain. The square's two other museums both have attractive courtyards and cool interiors. The **Museo de Arqueología Guamuhaya** (Sat–Thu 9am–5pm) in a beautiful mansion on the west side of the square traces pre- and post-Columbian history. The **Museo de Arquitectura Colonial** (Sat–Thu 9am–5pm) on the east side has examples of woodwork, ironwork, stained glass and other items culled from colonial houses. A block to the north of the Plaza Mayor in a former convent is the **Museo Nacional de Lucha Contra Bandidos** (National

The old town in Trinidad

Museum of the Struggle against Counter-Revolutionaries; Tue–Sun 9am–5pm), which documents the campaign to weed out rebels who hid in the Escambray mountains in the 1960s. The 360-degree view from the yellow belltower is the big draw.

A block south of Plaza Mayor on Calle Simón Bolívar stands the grand Palacio Cantero, built in 1830. Painted pillars, scrolls, shells, pediments and drapes embellish the interior, eclipsing the historical artefacts and old furniture that now form the **Museo Municipal de Historia** (Sat–Thu 9am–5pm). It has its own fine tower, though climbing its rickety narrow stairs can be a trial if a group has arrived there first.

A block south of the Plaza Mayor are two streets completely given over to sellers of handmade lace and other crafts. Further afield, southeast along Calle José Mendoza, you'll find the evocative ruins of **Iglesia de Santa Ana**, and overlooking the town from the north is the **Ermita La Papa**, a bricked-up

School children make their way home

church, on a hill where boys fly homemade kites.

Aimless wandering is especially fruitful in Trinidad – and, since dozens of street names have changed and neither maps nor residents seem sure of what to call many of them, roaming without a plan is the only practical solution. Virtually every street has its own colonial treasure and feast for the eyes.

Playa Ancón

## Around Trinidad

Trinidad's prosperity in the 19th century came from the fruits of 50 sugar mills nearby in the scenic **Valle de los Ingenios** 🔟 (Valley of the Sugar Mills), along with Trinidad a Unesco World Heritage Site. A *mirador* (lookout) with spectacular views is just 5km (3 miles) out of town. About 10km (6 miles) further east is Manaca-Iznaga, where you can explore a lovely colonial hacienda house and its startling, rocket-shaped *Torre de Manaca-Iznaga*. From the top of the tower, the Iznaga family would keep watch over their slaves toiling in the fields. Tours are available with the tour operators in Trinidad or you could arrange a taxi tour. A steam train once used in the sugar industry traverses the whole valley for tourists. It leaves from Estación Dragones, the station in the south of Trinidad, at 9.30am and returns at 2–3pm, CUC$10, but make sure you arrive at least 15 minutes before departure.

**Playa Ancón** 🔘, approximately 16km (10 miles) from Trinidad has an excellent strip of white sand and clear waters. Here you'll find diving at an offshore coral reef, a good choice of watersports and three mid-range hotels whose bars and sun-beds are available to all. Sunworshippers tend to congregate here, where there is a car park which serves as a transport hub. In high season there is an unreliable bus service, but there are also taxis and *cocotaxis*, or you can rent bicycles in town. Another good beach excursion is the day sail to the tiny island of **Cayo Blanco** from Playa Ancón, which should be organised through a tour operator.

## Sierra del Escambray

More compact than the island's eastern and western ranges, the **Sierra del Escambray** (Escambray mountains), coated in luxuriant vegetation, are arguably Cuba's most beautiful range and easily accessible. Blessed with their own microclimate, the mountains are a wonderfully cool refuge from the heat of Trinidad.

To get to the Topes de Collantes 🔞 national park, take the road west of Trinidad for the steep 15km (9-mile) climb through dense forests of palms, eucalyptus and pines. You'll pass a health resort, a Stalinesque complex that has decent facilities but lacks life. Two excellent hiking trails conclude with beautiful waterfalls: Salto de Caburní, at 62m (203ft), and Salto Vega Grande. Wear sturdy shoes, as each hike is a steep trek of 4km (2.5 miles) along a narrow and often muddy trail. You can swim in the chilly natural pools underneath the falls. Jeep excursions can be hired at any tour agency in Trinidad. There's a CUC$9 national park charge.

## Sancti Spíritus

Approximately 80km (50 miles) east of Trinidad is **Sancti Spíritus** 🔞, one of Diego Velázquez's seven original townships. Although no match for Trinidad, it has some attractive colonial buildings. The **Iglesia Parroquial Mayor del Espíritu Santo** has foundations from 1522, making it the country's oldest (though the present stone church was built in 1680). Nearby is the **Puente Yayabo**, the only remaining colonial stone arched bridge in Cuba.

## Santa Clara

A must on the itinerary of all fans of the Revolution, **Santa Clara ⑳** is a pleasant university city famous as the last resting place of guerrilla hero, Che Guevara. It was the site of the last battle, which started on 28 December 1958 and finished when news arrived that Batista had fled the country on 1 January 1959. An armoured troop train was heading

Cayo Guillermo

from Havana to Santiago, but Che and his men ambushed it at Santa Clara. Four of the carriages are preserved at the **Monumento a la Toma del Tren Blindado** (Calle Independencia; Mon–Sat 8am–6pm). You can go into the carriages and see some of the items carried on the train, as well as photos. At the **Plaza de la Revolución Ernesto Guevara** is a huge statue of Che in battle dress, while underneath is the **Mausoleum** (Tue–Sun 9am–5pm; free) where Che and his comrades who fell in battle in Bolivia in 1967 were interred when their remains were brought back in 1997. Next to it is the **Museo Histórico de la Revolución** (same hours as the Mausoleum), which has displays detailing Che's life and his role in the Revolution.

## Cayo Coco and Cayo Guillermo

These two offshore cays are reached by a causeway across the Bahía de Perros so long (28km/17 miles) that you can't see the land at the far end as you set off.

**Cayo Coco** ㉑ is named not for coconuts but for a bird: the ibis, as revealed in Hemingway's *Islands in the Stream*. The author patrolled these shores in World War II on the lookout for Nazis. Ibises and other wading birds, often pink flamingoes, can be seen balancing in the brackish waters around the principal causeway and a smaller causeway connecting the cay to **Cayo Guillermo**.

It's the impossibly white sandy beaches, the intensely blue waters, and the excellent fishing that draw holidaymakers, and there's not much else to distract you. Both cays are covered in forest or thick undergrowth. Large, luxury, all-inclusive resorts line the 22km (14 miles) of shell-shaped beaches on Cayo Coco. A wide range of non- motorised watersports are available to hotel guests. If you hire a moped or Jeep from your hotel, there are virgin beaches to discover, though with increased development they are fast disappearing.

## Camagüey

About 550km (342 miles) southeast of Havana, **Camagüey** ㉒ is an attractive colonial city; Cuba's third largest. Having been razed by Henry Morgan in 1668, it was rebuilt, with its narrow, twisting streets radiating haphazardly from the Hatibonico River as if to deter further pirate invasions. There are some half-dozen squares dotted around, each with an old church. Some, like Nuestra Señora del Carmen and Iglesia San Juan de Dios, have been nicely restored. The province's cattle-grazed plains hold little water, so the citizens fashioned huge earthenware pots to catch rainwater. Called *tinajones*, these still adorn many squares.

The city's most famous son, Ignacio Agramonte (1841–73), a general killed in battle in the Ten Years' War, was born here and his birthplace on Plaza de los Trabajadores is now a museum: **Museo Casa Natal de Ignacio Agramonte** (Avenida Agramonte 459, Tue–Sat 9am–5pm, Sun 8am– noon), a handsome, early 19th-century mansion. **Nuestra Señora de la Merced** church opposite has benefited from recent restoration: the decorated ceiling is particularly striking.

A dashing equine statue of Agramonte forms the centrepiece of **Parque Agramonte**, just to the south. The cathedral occupies one side of the park, and the Casa de la Trova, around a floral patio, has musical performances afternoon and evening.

A 10-minute walk west down Calle Cristo brings you to a dignified 18th-century church, **Santo Cristo del Buen Viaje**. Behind the church is a great sea of crosses and marble saints in a picturesque cemetery. A few blocks north is the triangular-shaped **Plaza del Carmen**, which has been beautifully restored and is notable for the life-size statues of local people passing

Catching up with the news in Plaza del Carmen, Camagüey

Dining al fresco in Camagüey

the time of day. In one corner stands the **Convento de Nuestra Señora del Carmen**; dating from the early 19th century, the restored church façade is one of the most beautiful in Cuba and is unique in Camagüey for having two towers.

Another splendid feature of Camagüey – and marvellously restored – is **Plaza San Juan de Dios**, an angular old cobblestoned square surrounded by brightly hued single-storey buildings dating from the 18th century, plus a lovely yellow church with a fine mahogany ceiling and altar, alongside a restored former hospital. It's one of Cuba's most beautiful plazas. A few blocks south, near the river, is an impressive agricultural market. A lively place, it's open every day and stocked with a surprising array of meat and fresh produce.

## Playa Santa Lucía

An hour-and-a-half drive (110km/68 miles) from Camagüey on the north coast, remote **Playa Santa Lucía ㉓** beckons sun worshippers with mid-range resort hotels strung along a particularly fine peninsular strip of sand. Each hotel backs directly onto the beach. A superb coral reef lies offshore, and diving here is excellent. Aside from a couple of roadside bars, however, nightlife is limited to hotel entertainment.

To counter the isolation of Playa Santa Lucía, the tourist authorities offer a wide range of excursions, including a rodeo at Rancho King, deep-sea fishing, and boat and helicopter trips for days on the beach at such unspoiled cays as Cayo Sabinal and Cayo Saetía.

A bus service visits **Playa Los Cocos**, some 5km (3 miles) away; with sheltered aquamarine waters, it's a strong contender for the title of 'Cuba's most beautiful beach'. Adjacent is La Boca, a very small community of waterside shacks with fish restaurants.

## ORIENTE: THE EAST

Prior to the Revolution, the east of Cuba was a single province known simply as **Oriente** ('East'), and most Cubans still refer to the region with this name. Oriente incorporates the post-revolutionary provinces of Holguín, Granma, Santiago de Cuba and Guantánamo, which are scenically and historically more interesting than most of central Cuba. The stunning

Mirador de Mayabe, Holguín

landscapes vary from the north coast's exuberant banana and coconut groves clustered round thatched huts, little changed from earlier indigenous peoples' *bohíos*, to the towering peaks of the Sierra Maestra mountains and lush rainforest on the east coast. Some of Cuba's best beaches lie on the north coast of Oriente within sight of the mountains.

The wars of independence began in Oriente in the 1860s, and nearly a century later Castro concentrated his power base in the inaccessible Sierra Maestra. There are stirring monuments and museums recalling these periods in Santiago de Cuba, the latter dubbed a 'heroic city' for its many historic patriots.

The further east you travel in Cuba the more Caribbean it feels. Santiago de Cuba is renowned for its contributions to Cuban musical culture; the Oriente is the heartland of son, the traditional rural music that formed the roots of salsa, and many of the genre's greats (Trío Matamoros, La Vieja Trova Santiaguera and Elíades Ochoa, among others) got their start in Santiago.

## Holguín Province

The province of Holguín begins bleakly around the busy capital but improves considerably as you travel north, where the countryside is lusher. **Guardalavaca ㉔**, 60km (37 miles) from Holguín, is an attractive resort, ringed by banana plantations. Watersports are excellent here and at the equally picturesque – but isolated – **Playa Esmeralda**, 2km (1 mile) west. All-inclusive hotels are dotted along the coast to the west, occupying horseshoe bays and sandy beaches such as

Playa Esmeralda

Playa Pesquero Viejo and Playa Pesquero Nuevo.

There are plenty of possibilities for excursions in the vicinity of Guardalavaca. You can take a boat trip into the middle of Bahía de Naranjo to a simple aquarium, or arrange sailing and fishing trips from the marina. To the west is **Bahía de Bariay**, which has a monument claiming Columbus's landing (a fact contested chiefly by Baracoa, further east). Beyond the bay is **Gibara**  ㉕ (27km/17 miles north of Holguín), a captivating if sleepy little port town, known for its annual festival for low-budget films.

Making music in Santiago

About 6km (4 miles) south of Guardalavaca, on a hill amid a forest of palms and thatched homesteads, is **Chorro de Maita** ㉖ (Tue–Sun 9am–5pm), the Caribbean's most important excavated pre-Columbian burial ground. Fifty-six of the 108 skeletons found are on display. They date from 1490 to 1540 and lie exactly as they were found. All but one are Amerindian, buried in the Central American style with arms folded across stomachs. The one Spaniard lies in a Christian fashion with arms crossed on his chest.

Banana groves coat the hillsides along the scenic 30km (19-mile) route south to **Banes** ㉗, a town of wooden houses with corrugated roofs. Castro was married at the church here in 1948, and the town's interesting **Museo Indo-Cubano Bani**

(Tue–Sat 9am–5pm, Sun 8am–noon, 2–5pm, Fri–Sun also 7–9pm) has some fascinating finds from the area.

## Santiago de Cuba

Many visitors prefer Cuba's second city (population 405,000) to the capital. **Santiago de Cuba** ❷⓼ (880km/546 miles southeast of Havana) is one of the oldest cities, with a wealth of colonial buildings. Unfailingly vibrant and seductive, it exudes a feel all its own. Enclosed by the Sierra Maestra mountains, Santiago can also be wickedly hot. *Santiagueros* negotiate their hilly streets by keeping to the shady sides, and they relax on overhanging balconies.

Santiago is Cuba's melting pot, with a friendly population of predominantly mulatto people: descendants of Spanish, French from Haiti, Jamaicans and huge numbers of African slaves. Afro-Cuban traditions remain strong, reflected in *carnaval*, which is still Cuba's best, and in music (walk down any street and a cacophony of sounds will emanate everywhere).

Founded in 1514, Santiago was the island's capital until 1553. It is regarded as a 'heroic city' (*ciudad héroe*), and locals are proud of the city's rebellious past. Seminal events brought it centre-stage again during the 1950s, when it assumed a major role in the revolutionary struggle. The attack on Batista's forces at the Moncada Barracks in 1953 thrust Fidel Castro into the national limelight, and it was in Santiago's main square that he first declared victory, on 1 January 1959.

### Old Santiago

The most atmospheric part of the city is **Old Santiago**. Castro delivered his victory speech in the heart of the old town, from the balcony of city hall on **Parque Céspedes**. The attractive square is a genteel place with tall trees, gas lanterns and iron benches. Old Santiago's grid of streets unfolds here, a few blocks inland from the heavily industrialised harbour. Parque Céspedes

Vintage car on a Santiago back street

is dominated by its twin-towered **cathedral**. A basilica was built on this spot in 1528, but what you see was rebuilt in the early 19th century after a series of earthquakes and fires.

On the west side of the plaza is **Casa de Diego Velázquez** (Mon–Thu and Sat 9am–5pm, Fri 2–5pm, Sun 9am–1pm). Noticeable for its black-slatted balconies, it was built in 1516 as the residence of the founder of Cuba's original seven *villas* (towns). The oldest house in Cuba and one of the oldest in the Americas, it is in remarkable condition. Housing the **Museo de Ambiente Histórico Cubano**, its rooms overflow with period furniture and carved woodwork and encircle two lovely courtyards. Across the square is the elegant **Hotel Casa Granda**, which opened in 1914 and hosted many celebrity guests and gangsters before the Revolution. Its terrace bar on the fifth floor affords excellent views of the cathedral towers and the city beyond.

East from the square, **Calle Heredia** is the epicentre of Santiago culture and tourism. The city's famous **Casa de la**

Museo de Ambiente
Histórico Cubano

**Trova** (music hall), which has hosted nearly all legendary Cuban musicians, is the centrepiece of both. Starting in midmorning, a succession of groups perform every style of Cuban music here, from *son* and *guarachas* to *boleros* and *salsa*. The intimate open-air space inside is the place to be in the evenings; at night the main groups play upstairs. Calle Heredia is lined by day with artisans and souvenir sellers.

Down the street is the **Museo El Carnaval** (Tue–Sun 9am–5pm), a museum containing instruments, photos and artefacts from Santiago's carnival. It also has Afro-Cuban music and dance (Sun–Fri at 4pm), as does the Artex store up the street. Also on Calle Heredia is the **Casa Natal de José María Heredia** (Tue–Sun 9am–5pm), the birthplace of the early 19th-century Cuban poet and a cultural centre and museum. A block south on Calle Bartolomé Masó, 358 (also called San Basilio) is the **Museo del Ron** (daily 9am–9pm), which explains the history of rum in Santiago and has an atmospheric bar for a post-tour rum tasting.

Nearby, on Calle Pío Rosado, the **Museo Provincial Emilio Bacardí** (Tue–Sat 9am–5.15pm, Sun 9am–12.15pm) has an excellent collection of Cuban art, as well as some European works, some items from the wars of independence and an archaeological hall that features a 3,000-year-old Egyptian mummy, two Peruvian skeletons and a shrunken head. The museum, in a grandiose neoclassical building on a beguiling little street, is named for its benefactor and the town's former mayor, whose family founded the Bacardí rum empire.

One of Santiago's most delightful people-watching spots is **Plaza Dolores**, a shady plaza lined with colonial-era homes (several now house tourist restaurants). **Avenida José A. Saco** (more commonly known as **Enramada**) is Santiago's main shopping thoroughfare. Its faded 1950s neon signs and ostentatious buildings recall more prosperous times. Cobbled **Calle Bartolomé Masó** (also known as San Basilio), just behind Heredia and the cathedral, is a delightful street that leads down to the picturesque Tivolí district.

In Tivolí you'll find the famous **Padre Pico** steps, named for a Santiaguero priest who aided the city's poor. Castro once roared fire and brimstone down on the Batista government here, but today you'll find more pacific chess and domino players who have set up all-hours tables on the steps. Take the steps up to the **Museo de la Lucha Clandestina**, the Museum of the Clandestine Struggle (Tue–Sun 9am–5pm). This excellent museum, in one of the city's finest colonial houses, focuses on the activities of the resistance movement under local martyr Frank País. Residents of Santiago were instrumental in supporting the Revolution, as were peasants in the Sierra Maestra. From the museum's balcony, there are tremendous views of Santiago and the bay (and, unfortunately, of plumes of pollution rising up from factories).

South of the museum is one of Santiago's best places to get sweaty in the evening.

## Bacardí's bat

Bacardí moved its headquarters and production to Puerto Rico after the Revolution, and from there to Bermuda. But it was the fruit bats that nested in the rafters of the original rum factory in Santiago that gave Bacardí rum its world-famous bat logo.

The **Casa de las Tradiciones**, a 'cultural centre' in a large colonial mansion with a central courtyard (Calle Jesús Rabí), has live *trova* and dancing. Known locally as La Casona, it's great fun, and local people usually outnumber tourists. Couples only.

## Around Santiago

A good place to get your bearings on the suburbs of the city is from the rooftop bar of the lavish hotel Meliá Santiago, 3km (almost 2 miles) east of the city's centre. In the near distance you can make out the yellow **Moncada Barracks**, which Castro, along with around 100 rebels attacked on 26 July 1953. The date is now a rallying cry and public holiday, and the barracks have been converted into a school and museum, known both as the **Antiguo Cuartel Moncada** and the **Museo Histórico 26 de Julio** (Av. Moncada esq. Gen. Portuondo; Tue–Sat 9am–7pm, Mon–Sun 9am–12.30pm; guided tour available in Spanish, English, French or Italian).

The museum tells the story of the road to revolution using dozens of memorable photographs. Also on display are various bloodstained rebel uniforms, some of Fidel's personal effects from his time in the mountains, and '26 Julio' armbands (sporting the name of the resistance movement that developed after the Moncada attack). The bullet holes over the entrance were 'restored' from photos.

North of Moncada, by the bus station, is the **Plaza de la Revolución**, an open square at the corner of Av. las Américas and Av. de los Libertadores. Massive machetes (used by *mambí* independence fighters) thrust towards the sky in this monument to Antonio Maceo, a hero of the war of independence, who is seen riding triumphantly.

The fine **Cementerio Santa Ifigenia**, just north of the harbour (Av. Crombet, Reparto Juan Gómez), is the resting place of many Cuban heroes. Pride of place goes to the Cuban founding father José Martí, in a vast octagonal mausoleum designed so that the tomb catches the sun throughout the day. An armed guard is changed ceremoniously every half hour. Céspedes is buried here too, as are the remains of 38 of the martyrs of the 26 July movement. They are interred in a wall just inside the entrance; each 'brick' is marked with a name.

In an impressive setting 7km (4 miles) from the city is the 17th-century **Castillo del Morro** (daily 9am–7pm), surveying the harbour mouth from a commanding clifftop position.

Plaza de la Revolución

Moated, thick-walled, and full of cannons, drawbridges and passageways, it is in fine condition. A guide will point out a torture room with a trap door in the floor, through which uncooperative prisoners and slaves were reportedly dropped into the sea below. The restaurant near the fortress, also called 'El Morro', has gorgeous views of the sea and some of Santiago's finest food. The easiest way to get to El Morro is to hire a taxi, which costs around CUC$25 for the round trip.

A place of great import (and considerable beauty) is the triple-domed **Basílica del Cobre** ㉙ (daily 7am–6pm; taxi from Santiago around CUC$20–30 round trip) named after the nearby copper mines that rise out of the forested foothills

Basílica del Cobre

18km (11 miles) west of Santiago. Cuban faithful make annual pilgrimages to the church to pay tribute to its statue of a black virgin, the Virgen de la Caridad (Virgin of Charity), Cuba's patron saint. According to legend, in 1606 three young fishermen struggling in their storm-tossed boat out in the bay were saved by the miraculous appearance of the Virgin, who was holding a mulatto baby Jesus in one hand and a cross in the other. Pilgrims, often making the last of the trek on their knees, pray to her image and place memen-tos and offerings of thanks for her miracles; among them are small boats and prayers for those who have tried to escape Cuba on rafts. Except during Mass, the Virgin is kept on the second floor, encased in glass and cloaked in a glitter-ing gold robe.

Day trips are offered by tour operators in Santiago up into the Sierra Maestra. Some go to **El Saltón**, a picturesque water-fall in the grounds of a small hotel. Alternatively you can hike up Pico Turquino (1,974m/ 6,476ft), the highest mountain.

East of Santiago is **Parque Baconao**, a biosphere reserve spread over 40km (25 miles). The local dark-sand beaches can be scrubby and the hotels themselves are isolated, but there's lots to explore in the park, and the Sierra de La Gran Piedra rises majestically above the coast. A tortuous side road 12km

(7 miles) east along the coast ascends the mountains to **La Gran Piedra ③** (Great Stone), where you can climb on foot for a bird's-eye view of eastern Cuba. About 2km (1 mile) beyond, a track leads to the **Cafetal-Museo La Isabelica**, a 19th-century coffee-plantation *finca* (country house). The museum (Mon–Sat 9am–5pm) is part of the Unesco World Heritage Site that protects the architectural legacy of early 19th-century coffee farms.

## GUANTÁNAMO PROVINCE

You can reach Cuba's remote, mountainous, far-eastern region from Santiago. The province has only one true tourist draw, but it's a super one: the magical little town of Baracoa. The only reason to stop near the unappealing city of Guantánamo would be to visit the lookout point trained on the US naval base with its controversial Camp Delta detention centre, built in 2002 to hold foreign terror suspects captured during the war against the Taliban and Al Qaeda in Afghanistan. To visit the Mirador de Malones lookout, you must arrange your trip in advance through one of the central tour agencies in Santiago, who issue vouchers for entry. The

### 'Gitmo'

Guantánamo, known to American military personnel as 'Gitmo', is a curious anomaly in revolutionary Cuba. Where in the world is the US less likely to have a military base? Established in 1903 – making it the oldest overseas American naval base – the lease was effectively forced on the Cubans by an interventionist US administration. The US still sends its annual rent cheques (about US$4,000), which haven't been cashed since 1960. To do so would be to recognise the legitimacy of the American presence in Cuba.

lookout can be visited en route to Baracoa; there is no need to overnight in Guantánamo.

## Baracoa

The dry, cactus-strewn landscape of the south coast begins to change as you follow the winding, spectacular 30km (18-mile) road 'La Farola' across the mountains to **Baracoa** ③① (150km/93 miles from Santiago), a picturesque little village known for its local chocolate and coconut factories. The tropical seaside town is surrounded by green hillsides covered with cocoa and coconut groves, and all around are palm-backed beaches. Baracoa lies smack in the middle of the wettest region in Cuba, and has no fewer than 10 rivers, all of them ripe for whitewater rafting. In the mountains to the northwest is the Parque Nacional Alejandro de Humboldt, a biosphere reserve named after the great German naturalist and explorer.

Baracoa: first Spanish settlement on Cuba, famous for its rain

Baracoa was the first settlement to be established by Diego Velázquez in 1511. Columbus came here first, though, after landing at Bariay Bay in today's Holguín province in October 1492, and planted the Cruz de la Parra (Cross of the Vine) in the soil on his arrival. What is claimed to be this cross is on display in **Nuestra Señora de la Asunción**, the church on Plaza Independencia.

### Festive day

Baracoa really shines the week of 1 April, when heady street parties every night commemorate the date General Antonio Maceo disembarked at nearby Playa Duaba in 1895, marking the beginning of Cuba's War of Independence.

A good place to get your bearings is the hilltop **Hotel El Castillo**, a former castle looking out over red-tiled roofs, the town's expansive, oyster-shaped bay and the landmark mountain called El Yunque (The Anvil), named for its singular shape.

In the main square is a bust of Hatuey, the brave Indian leader who resisted early *conquistadores* until he was caught by the Spanish and burned at the stake. There's also a very lively Casa de la Trova here. It is worth wandering along the Malecón, the seaside avenue, from the snug **Fuerte Matachín** (an early 19th century fort that has a small but informative municipal museum inside, daily 8am–6pm) to the Hotel La Rusa, which is named after a legendary Russian émigrée who over the years hosted celebrities such as Che Guevara and Errol Flynn.

In and around Baracoa are several dozen pre-Columbian archaeological sites related to the two major indigenous groups that once inhabited the region. The **Museo Arqueológico** (Mon–Fri 8am–5pm, Sat 8am–noon) in **Las Cuevas del Paraíso** up the hill from the village, contains a copy of the Taíno tobacco idol found nearby in 1903 (the original is in Havana).

# WHAT TO DO

## ENTERTAINMENT

Although cultural activity has been under state control since the revolution and Havana no longer sizzles with the sleazy Mafia-funded casinos and clubs of the 1950s, both high culture and down-to-earth nightlife thrive in Cuba. Outside the resorts, it can be hard to pin down what's going on where, but informal musical performances are ubiquitous. In the resorts, nightlife is focused around hotels, ranging from decent live bands, dance and fashion shows to Beatles sing-alongs.

### Live Music Performances

Cubans crave live music, and – with the surge in international popularity of traditional Cuban music – so do most visitors to Cuba. You certainly won't have to go out of your way to hear music performances. Roving groups of musicians can be found playing everywhere from airports to restaurants. Merely wandering the streets of Havana, Santiago or Trinidad, you're likely to stumble across a party with a live band, or even a back alley where some impromptu jamming is going on.

All the styles of Cuba's traditional music – *habaneras, son, boleros, guarachas, guajiras* and more   can be heard in every town's *casa de la trova*, usually a fine old building on or near the main square. Performances take place afternoons and evenings. Especially in the evenings and on weekends, the island's *casas de la trova* really swing. The most famous is in Santiago de Cuba, while those in towns like Trinidad, Baracoa, Camagüey and Holguín are great fun.

Local musicians in Havana

Aside from traditional acoustic music, Cuba revels in salsa. In Havana the salsa dance fan can choose from a number of venues every night. They feature top salsa groups, but cover charges are still quite low. Music hotspots include:

**Havana**. Casa de la Música Egrem (all types of music and dance including salsa; Avenida 35 and Calle 20, Miramar), Casa de la Música Galiano (lots of variety from rock to salsa, new bands and established big names; Calle Galiano 255,

## A Musical Melting Pot

Salsa, rumba, mambo, *cha-cha-chá*, son, *danzón*–Cuba's rhythms are known the world over. Reflecting the mixed heritage of its people, Cuban music spontaneously combusted towards the end of the 1800s through the nexus of African and European cultures – in particular what's been described as the love affair between the African drum and the Spanish guitar. In a typical Cuban band today you'll hear Latin stringed instruments in harmony with congas, *timbales* and African bongos (all drums), *claves* (wooden sticks) and instruments made from hollow gourds such as the maracas and the *güiro*. Cuban percussionists are among the finest in the world.

First came *son* ('sound'), a style that originated in Oriente around the turn of the 20th century. Son permeates all Cuban music and is the direct forebear of salsa; it has a percussive swing that is intrinsically Cuban. Mixed with jazz influences, it led to the brass-band salsa of famous groups such as Los Van Van, Isaac Delgado and Irakere. *Cha-cha-chá* arrived in the 1950s, having developed from mambo, itself a blend of jazz and the sedate, European *danzón* of the ballroom. The strongly Afro-Cuban rumba is typified by heavy drumming and more celebratory, erotic dancing. *Trovas* (ballads) were sung in colonial times by troubadors in *casas de la trova*. After the revolution the *trova* evolved into the *nueva trova*, often with overtly political lyrics, made popular by such artists as Silvio Rodríguez and Pablo Milanés.

e/ Concordia y Neptuno, Centro), Teatro Nacional – El Delirio Habanero (piano bar, *nueva trova*, dancing to live band or disco; 5th floor, Paseo y Calle 39, Plaza de la Revolución) and Café Cantante (dancing to live bands or disco, often top bands; in the basement) and la Zorra y el Cuervo (jazz; Calles 23 y O, Vedado).

Getting the salsa rhythm

**Trinidad**. Casa de la Trova (traditional music; Fernando Echerri 29, e/ Jesús Menéndez y Patricio Lumumba), Casa de la Música (two venues on the Escalinata near the Plaza Mayor), Palenque de los Congos Reales (Afro-Cuban folkloric show during the day, son and salsa at night; Fernando Echerri half a block away towards the Plaza Mayor).

**Santiago de Cuba**. Casa de la Trova (*trova*, son and boleros, famous musicians play here; Calle Heredia), Casa de las Tradiciones (*trova*, son and boleros; Calle Rabí 154).

**Baracoa**. Casa de la Trova (Via Felix Ruene) and Casa de la Cultura (Maceo, 124).

## Cabaret

A legacy of the high-rolling casino days in Cuba, cabarets have been kept alive and well as a magnet for tourist spending. Cavorting mulatta dancers in sparkling G-strings and pairs of strategically placed stars may not be most peoples' image of socialist doctrine – but this is Caribbean communism.

While the best shows (at the Tropicana clubs in both Havana and Santiago de Cuba) are rather expensive by Cuban standards, seeing at least one big song-and-dance production in the flesh (so to speak) is de rigueur.

The **Tropicana in Havana** (Calle 72 #4504 e/ 43 y 45, Marianao, tel: 07-267 1717; http://tropicanacabaret.com), founded in 1939, is indisputably the queen of cabarets. The likes of Nat King Cole performed here in pre-revolutionary times. With a 32-piece orchestra and a cast of over 200, in a dazzling open-air arena, the sheer scale of the spectacle will make your head spin. Tickets cost from CUC\$70–90, including a quarter bottle of rum and a mixer. Book at your hotel reception or buy tickets at the entrance between 8.30 and 9pm. The show starts at 10pm and lasts 1 hour 45 minutes, after which you can head to the club. Havana's next-best cabaret show, smaller and half the price, is Cabaret Parisien, at the Hotel Nacional (Calles 21 and O, Vedado, tel: 07-873 3564; nightly at 10pm).

The **Tropicana in Santiago de Cuba** (Autopista Nacional km 1.5; tel: 22-642 579) fills an enormous complex on the city's northern outskirts. It is no less impressive than Havana's but tickets are less expensive (CUC\$30 or group packages with transport and one drink included CUC\$44 per person); get there for 9.30pm in time for the main show at 10pm.

## Dance

Afro-Cuban dance is often seen in resort hotels as part of the evening entertainment, but is best seen in theatres. The internationally renowned company, Clave y Guaguancó, perform Afro-Cuban dance, drumming and music and can be sometimes found performing in Callejón de Hamel (Centro Habana) on Sunday afternoons. The Conjunto Folklórico Nacional de Cuba puts on rumba performances outside the Gran Palenque Bar, Calle 4 e/ Calzada y 5, on

Saturday. Get there early, the box office opens at 2pm for a 3pm show.

The Ballet Nacional de Cuba was created in 1961 and has been supported by the Revolution ever since under the direction of prima ballerina Alicia Alonso. World famous and often on tour, when in Cuba they perform at the Gran Teatro on the Parque Central, Havana or the Teatro Nacional, Plaza de la Revolución. The Ballet de Camagüey is another classical ballet company, sometimes considered to be more innovative. Also worth seeing is the Danza Contemporánea de Cuba, which is based at the Teatro Nacional but also performs at other venues in Havana and nationwide.

Tropicana Cabaret performer, Havana

Visitors to Santiago de Cuba should try to see the Ballet Folklórico Cutumba, a renowned troupe that delves into the world of Afro-Cuban spirituality and ritual. They perform at several theatres when in town and also offer dance classes. At the Museo del Carnaval there is an Afro-Cuban dance show by the Orishas at 4pm.

## Discos
Discos pulsate to both Latin and Euro-American rhythms. The places to be are Habana Café (the disco in Havana's Hotel Meliá Cohiba) and the disco in

Santiago's eponymous hotel. These are glitzy affairs, where foreigners get merry and approached by hustlers of all stripes. Situated in an old peanut oil factory, trendy Fabrica de Arte Cubano (Calle 26 esq. 11, Vedado; www.fabricade artecubano.com) offers a unique blend of art, music, cinema, disco and dance. Expect long queues. Varadero has Palacio de La Rumba at the end of Avenue Las Américas, which is popular with a young crowd and has live salsa bands at weekends; or Mambo Club – on the Autopista Sur, further down the peninsula, by the Gran Hotel – which is similar but with live music.

Entrance is CUC$10 in both cases, but you get free national drinks at the bar. In Trinidad, the Discoteca Ayala Las Cuevas really gets going at 1am, when the other music venues in town close. In Guardalavaca, head for open-air La Roca, set just above the beach.

Preparing mojitos

## Bars and Cafés

Both bars and cafés are places to have a mojito, daiquiri or shot of *ron* (rum), smoke a Cohiba, and – usually – hear some live Cuban rhythms. In Havana the bars not to miss are Hemingway haunts: La Bodeguita del Medio and El Floridita. Enjoyable café-bars in Havana include Café de París (Obispo y San Ignacio), Café O'Reilly (O'Reilly y San Ignacio), Bolabana (Calle 39 esq. 50, Playa) and El Patio (Plaza de la Catedral). There are also several places on Plaza Vieja, including Cervecería Taberna de La Muralla with home-brewed malt beer; and on the opposite corner, the Café Taberna at Mercaderes esq. Teniente Rey, done up in 1950s style and dedicated to the late, great Cuban singer, Beny Moré. Several hotels also have good bars, including Hotel Sevilla (made famous in Graham Greene's *Our Man in Havana*), Hotel Inglaterra's rooftop bar and Hotel Havana Libre's Turquino (with amazing views from the 25th floor).

In Santiago de Cuba, the terrace bar on the fifth floor of the Hotel Casa Granda has fine views and live music. A good place for a cold beer is Taberna de Dolores, which often has live music in its courtyard. At the corner of Calle Calvario is Café Isabelica, a venerable 24-hour bohemian haunt in a house three centuries old. Baracoa's Hotel Castillo has a bar with sensational views and frequent live music.

## Classical Repertoire

The classical arts are greatly valued in Cuba, and drama, opera, classical music recitals and above all ballet can be enjoyed in theatres all around Cuba. Opulent, old-fashioned theatres such as those in Cienfuegos, Camagüey and Matanzas and Havana's magnificent Gran Teatro, are sights in their own right.

The Gran Teatro in Havana, at Prado y San José (tel: 3077), has two main concert halls and puts on a wide toire of entertainment, from opera recitals to ballet. It is to the internationally renowned Ballet Nacional de Cuba. Havana's International Ballet Festival is held every two years during the last week of October and first week of November.

At the Teatro Amadeo Roldán in Havana, at Calzada y D, Vedado, you can hear the Orquesta Sinfónica Nacional and visiting Symphony Orchestras. Other theatres and concert halls in Vedado include the Sala Hubert de Blanck, for classical and contemporary music concerts as well as drama and dance; Teatro El Sótano, for contemporary drama; Teatro Mella for modern dance and drama and Teatro Nacional de Cuba for concerts, drama and live bands in the Café Cantante and El Delirio Habanero. In 2014 the legendary Teatro Martí reopened, following a 40-year hiatus, with a programme of traditional Cuban music shows. Out in Miramar is the Teatro Karl Marx, used for grand occasions when large audiences can be accommodated.

Shopping in Havana

## SHOPPING

Cuba has a reputation as a destination where there's little worth buying. You will see incredibly barren shops – window displays with bottles of cooking oil, shoe polish and a few plumbing parts. But there are plenty of things for visitors to buy. The dual currency system means that you pay for your goods in *pesos convertibles* (CUCs), while Cubans pay for their basic goods in *pesos Cubanos*, or *moneda nacional* (CUPs). Top on most people's lists are Cuba's greatest achievements (not including its health care system): cigars, rum and music. There is also an excellent selection of handicrafts, and tourist markets are now thriving in Cuba's major centres, even if much of what you'll find is related to Che

## Export permits

If you purchase anything that can be described as art – even a cheap watercolour at a flea market – you'll need an official export permit to get it out of the country without hassle or fear of confiscation. Most official galleries should be able to provide you with this – a purchase receipt will not usually be sufficient.

Guevara – berets, T-shirts bearing his countenance, and dolls, among many other 'revolutionary' items.

As for essentials, hotel and dollar shops (as the CUC shops are still called) carry mineral water, soap, shampoo, toilet paper and toothpaste, and these items are now sometimes available from small kiosk shops. However, it's still best to bring all your medicinal or cosmetic staples from home. Tiendas Panamericanas and Caracol are well-stocked stores, but probably the most impressive store in all Cuba is the Harris Bros. Company, a multistorey enterprise near the landmark Art Deco Bacardí building and the Capitolio.

## Souvenirs to Buy

**Cigars and rum.** The biggest bargain in Cuba is probably a coveted box of premium cigars, which at home might cost four times more. Cigar factories have affiliated shops selling all brands of cigars; the Partagás factory in Havana has a particularly good shop, as does the specialist cigar hotel in Old Havana: Hostal Conde de Villanueva at Mercaderes 202. You can also purchase cigars at shops such as Casa del Tabaco (Calle Obispo and Bernaza) and La Casa del Habano (Calle

Cuba's finest cigars

Mercaderes, 120) in Havana, at hotels and at the airport. You will find Habanos shops in several other towns (Trinidad's is on Lino Pérez, 296).

Bottles of Cuban rum also offer big savings. All tourist shops sell rum, whether aged from three to seven years (*añejo*) or low-grade *aguardiente* (from sugarcane alcohol) with humorous labels. Havana Club is the brand of choice and aficionados should visit the distillery's **Museo del Ron** (Av. del Puerto, 262 e/ Sol y Muralla) for a tour and rum tasting, as well as the shop attached. Above El Floridita, Havana's Casa del Ron has the most impressive selection of rums, including hundred-dollar vintages.

**Music recordings**. CDs and cassettes of Cuban music are widely available. If you're in the market for Cuban recordings, look for the EGREM label, available in Artex stores (as well as others). Most are CUC$15 each. Recommended recordings include those by Trio Matamoros, Beny Moré, Celina González, La Vieja Trova Santiaguero, Los Compadres, Los Zafiros, El Cuarteto Patria, Los Van Van, Silvio Rodríguez, Chucho Valdés and Pablo Milanés, to name just a few of Cuba's most popular musicians.

**Handicrafts.** Local arts and crafts vary from tacky figurines to drawings of street scenes. You'll also find evocative posters and black-and-white photos of Fidel, Che and company. Fine handmade lace and crochet are available, principally in Trinidad. You might want to pick up a *guayabera*, the classic

# El Puro: The Cuban Cigar

Before launching the US trade embargo against Cuba, President Kennedy reportedly had an aide round up a supply of his favourite Cuban cigars. Now that cigars have again become chic, almost everyone knows that Cuban *puros* are reputed to be the world's finest. Factories produce more than 350 million cigars a year, with 100 million for export. Before the revolution there were more than 1,000 Cuban brands of cigars; today there are only about three dozen.

You can visit a number of cigar factories, where the rich aroma is overwhelming. *Torcedores* wrap the different types of leaves (some for taste, burn, etc) inside the wrapper leaves with dexterous ease. Sacks of tobacco leaves are sorted into bundles, cigars undergo quality control tests, and prestigious labels are applied. Handmade cigars vary in length from the 4.5-inch Demi Tasse to the 9.25-inch Gran Corona. As a rule, bigger cigars are of better quality and darker-coloured cigars taste sweeter. Back home, keep your cigars moist: place them in a humidor or put the box in a plastic bag with a damp sponge.

Buying a box of cigars can be daunting. People on the street will whisper 'You want cigar, my friend?' and tell you that their sister (or mother or cousin) works in the factory and that the cigars are stolen. They may be hot, but they may also be inferior-quality fakes. Don't buy unless you know what you're doing. In a shop, ask to look inside the box, take out a cigar, see if you like the aroma, and check for uniform colour. The cigars should be slightly springy.

Fakes are liable to confiscation by customs. In official shops, make sure you keep the two copies of the official receipt – one of these is for you and one is to be given to customs when leaving the country. Keep cigars in your hand luggage for inspection. You are allowed to take up to 20 loose cigars and up to 50 in their original sealed packaging, with the official hologram, out of the country without a receipt.

Cuban pleated, four-pocketed man's shirt, worn untucked. Boutique Quitrín (Obispo esq. San Ignacio in Old Havana) has the nicest cotton versions of the original white *guayabera*. Much of the silver-plated jewellery is also a good buy, but you should not purchase anything with black coral – it's endangered and illegal to import in many countries.

There are more interesting things to buy in Old Havana than in the rest of Cuba put together. A lively crafts market (daily 9am–5pm) is held next to ferry terminal on Desamparados. Plaza de Armas is busy with second-hand booksellers. The excellent Palacio de la Artesanía (at Calle Cuba, 64 e/ Peña Pobre y Cuarteles; open daily 10am–5pm, Sun until 1pm) is a souvenir supermarket. Outside Havana, Trinidad has the best array of crafts shops in the country. Several streets just south of the Plaza Mayor (around the *Casa de la Trova*), known as La Candonga, stage a vibrant daily crafts market, and you'll find good government-run crafts shops on Simón Bolívar. Santiago de Cuba's crafts mecca is among the shops and vendors along Calle Heredia.

# SPORTS

## Watersports

Watersports enthusiasts are in luck in Cuba. Virtually every resort offers windsurfing, sailing, scuba diving and snorkelling. As anywhere in the world, motorised sports are expensive. Watersports centres are almost always affiliated with a particular hotel, but anyone may rent the equipment.

**Diving** is the area of greatest interest and growth. Cuba claims to be surrounded by one of the world's largest coral reefs, and over 1,000 sunken wrecks. Facilities are generally excellent, and prices are the lowest in the Caribbean. Nearly every resort has at least one professional diving centre

Snorkeling at María la Gorda

equipped with all the requisite equipment. Most centres offer week-long diving courses for an internationally recognised qualification, as well as two-day introductory courses.

Dozens of dive sites can be reached from resorts, typically a half-hour boat journey away. The diving centre at El Colony Hotel on the Isla de la Juventud offers the best facilities and diving, but it isn't well suited to beginners. Resorts catering to all levels of ability include Playa Santa Lucía, María la Gorda, Cayo Levisa, Cayo Largo, Varadero, Playa Girón, Playa Ancón, Cayo Coco and Guardalavaca.

**Deep-sea fishing** is one of Cuba's great attractions, as of yet not well known (or over-fished). Trips in search of marlin, wahoo, swordfish and tarpon or smaller fry can be arranged through **Marlin Naútica y Marinas** (www.nauticamarlin. com) around the island at the Marina Hemingway, Marina Tarará, Varadero, Cayo Guillermo, Cayo Coco, Santa Lucía, Guardalavaca, Marina Santiago de Cuba, Marina Trinidad,

Young baseball player

Marina Cienfuegos, Jardines de la Reina, Isla de la Juventud and Cayo Largo del Sur. There is fly fishing in the Jardines de la Reina off the south coast, off Cayo Largo del Sur and in the salt flats of the Zapata peninsula. For **freshwater fishing**, Hanabanilla and Zaza (near Sancti Spíritus) lakes both hold impressively big, copious large-mouth bass, as do Maspotón in Pinar del Río, Laguna del Tesoro in the Zapata peninsula.

## Spectator Sports

The national sport is **baseball** *(béisbol)*. Cuban teams are among the best in the world (several stars have defected to the US major leagues). While children improvise with a stick and a makeshift ball in every town's open spaces, the main cities have vast stadiums.

## CUBA FOR CHILDREN

At resorts, water-loving babies will be happy; those aged 10 and up will be able to join in many of the activities. A few resort hotels (such as those at Cayo Coco) have children's clubs, and top hotels can arrange babysitting. Outside the resorts facilities are limited and transport can be problematic. Cubans adore children and will certainly make a fuss over yours. Travelling with young families in Cuba can be a remarkable – and eye-opening – experience. If you travel with very young children, be sure to take all the diapers and baby food you require, as these items are hard to find in Cuba. If travelling by hire car, you should supply your own car seat.

## Calendar of Events

The Buró de Convenciones (Hotel Neptuno, Calle 3 e/70 y 74, Miramar; tel: 7-204 8273) has information and contact details for all of the festivals and conferences held throughout the year all over the country.

**January** New Year (1 January, public holiday): celebrated throughout the country and taking in Liberation Day marking the end of the Batista dictatorship, with music, dancing and outdoor parties.

**May** May Day (1 May, public holiday): a big event with parades and speeches in all the Plazas de la Revolución in every town.

**June** Hemingway Marlin Fishing Tournament (Hemingway Marina, Havana): four-day competition begun in 1950 and won by Castro in 1960.

**July** (first week): Caribe Festival (Santiago de Cuba): street parades, concerts, lectures and fairs celebrating Afro-Caribbean culture.

**18–27 July** Carnaval (Santiago de Cuba): Cuba's most famous celebration, featuring comparsas (street dances), takes in Santiago's patron saint's day on the 25th, but stops temporarily on the 26th in memory of the attack on the Moncada barracks in 1953.

**August** Carnaval (Havana): parades, open-air concerts and street parties.

**8 September** Fiesta de la Virgen del Cobre: pilgrimage to the altar of Cuba's saint in El Cobre near Santiago de Cuba.

**October–November** Havana International Ballet Festival: a gathering of top ballet companies from around the world, begun in 1960 and held in alternate years.

**December** New Latin American Film Festival (Havana): the most important film festival in Latin America, held during the first two weeks of the month. International Jazz Festival (Havana): a week-long festival, which attracts top jazz artists from Cuba and around the world: performances, workshops, lectures and open rehearsals.

# EATING OUT

It is a sad paradox that a land as fertile as Cuba should have such problems feeding its people. During the so-called Special Period of the early 1990s, food shortages became serious and distribution of harvested fruit and vegetables remains a problem. Ration books no longer provide enough to live on and are expected gradually to be phased out, leaving poor Cubans with uncertainty. However, those with plenty of money (tourists and a small number of Cubans) are immune from hardships and get the most and best of what little is available. Nevertheless, do not come to Cuba expecting memorable gastronomic experiences. Cuba once had a respectable *criollo* (Creole) cuisine, a fusion of Spanish and African culinary traditions. But many Cubans now have been reduced to eating simple box lunches and sandwiches. Many restaurants have no choice but to offer standard 'chicken or pork' main courses, along with rice and beans. Most hotels play it safe by offering international fare.

## Where to Eat

If you're based in a resort, you might face the potentially monotonous reality of eating almost all your meals at the hotel. Large hotels often have not only a main buffet restaurant but also an à la carte restaurant, a poolside *parrillada* (grill) and a beachside café.

State-run restaurants are of two types. Those for which you must pay in pesos *convertibles*, and those for which *pesos cubanos* are the accepted currency. The latter are usually cafeteria style for Cubans, have extremely limited menus and, generally, are of poor quality with long waits. In some isolated cities (like Bayamo) it is possible to eat in *peso cubano* establishments very cheaply, as long as you understand that perhaps only one item on the menu will be available and that Cuban diners might look at you as if to say, 'How did you get in here?' Often, however, they will charge in *pesos convertibles* because you are a foreigner.

A third category is the *paladar*, a privately operated restaurant in a private home. These cater to anyone who pays in *pesos convertibles*. In 1995 the government legalised them, only to subsequently tax or fine many of them out of existence. In 2011 restrictions were relaxed in order to create jobs, allowing more to open, employ staff and increasing the maximum legal number of place settings from 12 to 50. The food is often better than in state-owned restaurants and the cost is more reasonable. You'll be offered a three-course meal, sometimes with a beer or juice included, for a set price. *Paladares* are like small, simple restaurants, usually with menus, that just happen to be on the terrace or in someone's home.

Tables outside El Patio restaurant, Havana

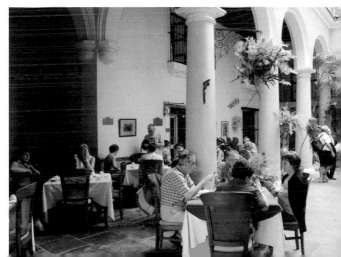

If you are staying at a *casa particular* (see page 133), you can take advantage of the freshest and best *criollo* food. Families will cook whatever you want, or offer a few staple dishes. Usually you decide in the morning whether you want to eat in and they will shop and cook it for your evening meal. Fortified by a hearty breakfast of fresh fruit, eggs, coffee, juice and bread, these two meals will probably be enough, with just a snack at midday.

In all resort hotels and around Havana, cafés serve sandwiches (almost always ham and/or cheese), but otherwise snacks in Cuba are limited to bad street pizza and box lunches. Picnic food is an even more difficult proposition: hotel shops sell packs of biscuits and chips, while private farmers' markets sell fruit for pesos.

## What to Eat

At large hotels, particularly in the resorts, breakfast can be the best meal of the day: a buffet of fresh fruit, fruit juices, cheeses, meats and pancakes. Often there are also egg dishes made to order. In more modest hotels, sandwiches and omelettes are generally the staple fare.

Fruit at a street market

Hotel buffets are also offered at lunch and dinner, and guests with large appetites will find these very good value. The food is 'international' rather than typically Cuban. The surfeit of choices (several salads, piles of bananas, chunks of watermelon, cakes galore, a choice of fish, meat and pasta) might make some travellers uncomfortable, given the limited supplies most Cubans put up with.

Most restaurants serve a Creole Cuban cuisine. Its main staple is rice and beans; you'll find either rice with kidney beans (*moros y cristianos*; 'Moors and Christians') or rice with black beans (*congrís*), the latter typically served in the east of Cuba. Meat is often *pollo asado* (roast chicken) or *cerdo asado* (roast pork). White fish is commonly presented under the generic label *pescado* and is typically fresh and simply grilled; numerous restaurants also serve lobster at a hefty price (CUC$25–30). Popular side dishes include

*Guarapo* (sugar cane juice)

root vegetables such as *malanga* and *yuca* (cassava) in addition to *maduros* or *tostones* (fried plantains). Common desserts are *pasta de guayaba con queso* (cheese with guava paste) and Coppelia ice cream, made all over the country.

## What to Drink

The national drink is *ron* (rum), produced from cane juice and molasses, the by-products of sugar manufacture. Un-aged rum, called *aguardiente* ('firewater'), has a very high alcoholic content. Five- or seven-year-old rum, darkened and flavoured in oak barrels, is drunk straight or on the rocks.

Cuban cocktails make use of one- or three-year-old white rum. A number have achieved folkloric status: Hemingway

Thirst-quencher: the mojito

drank his mojitos (sugar, lime juice, ice, fresh mint, rum and soda water) in La Bodeguita del Medio and his daiquiris (sugar, lime juice and rum blended into crushed ice) in El Floridita. Less exotic is the *Cuba libre*: simply rum and coke, served with a slice of lime.

National brands of beer include Bucanero, Cristal, Mayabe and Tínima, all very drinkable. Only the more expensive restaurants serve wine. Cuban wine is now produced with the help of Spanish technology, but is in its infancy and best avoided.

For soft drinks, try the wonderfully sweet *guarapo* (pure sugar cane juice) or *granizado* (a flavoured water-ice in a paper cone from ubiquitous streetside carts). In some towns, you may come across homemade cola stands, where they'll mix three shots of syrup with soda water. It's amazingly refreshing and only about 5 centavos.

Coffee is one of Cuba's main exports, but you don't always get export-quality coffee. In times of hardship it is mixed with chicory, a flavour many Cubans have got used to and now prefer. A *café* is served espresso style and traditionally drunk with unimaginable quantities of sugar; *café americano* is weaker and served in a large cup. *Café con leche* is half espresso/half milk. Coffee with a little cream in Cuba is often disappointingly grey.

## TO HELP YOU ORDER...

Do you have a table?. **¿Tiene una mesa?**
May I see the menu, please? **¿Puedo ver la carta, por favor?**
What do you recommend? **¿Qué me aconseja?**
I'd like ... **Quisiera ...**
I'm a vegetarian **Soy vegetariano.**

beer **cerveza**
bread **pan**
butter **mantequilla**
cocktail **cóctel**
coffee **café**
dessert **postre**
fish **pescado**
fruit **fruta**
ice **hielo**
ice cream **helado**

meat **carne**
salad **ensalada**
sandwich **bocadito**
shellfish **mariscos**
soft drink **refresco**
tea **té**
vegetable **vegetales/ legumbres**
water **agua mineral**
wine **vino**

## ...AND READ THE MENU

**arroz blanco** white rice
**asado** roast/grilled
**bistec** steak
**camarones** shrimps/ prawns
**cerdo/Puerco** pork
**congrí** rice and beans
**frijoles** beans
**frito** fried
**huevos** eggs
**jamón** ham

**jugo de fruta** fruit juice
**langosta** lobster
**naranja** orange
**pan tostado** toast
**papas** potatoes
**papas fritas** chips (fries)
**picadillo** minced meat
**platáno** plantain
**pollo** chicken
**queso** cheese
**tortilla/revoltillo** omelette

# PLACES TO EAT

*We have used the following symbols to give an idea of the price for a three-course meal for one, excluding drinks, tips and shellfish (the latter is always the costliest on the menu).*

**$$$** over CUC$25          **$$** CUC$12–25          **$** under CUC$12

## OLD HAVANA

**La Barca $$–$$$** *Avenida del Puerto esq Obispo, tel:* (7) 866 8807. Open daily noon–midnight. Overlooking the harbour and the old yacht club, this is a pleasant open-air restaurant in the Habaguanex chain serving good Spanish food with lots of seafood. Alongside is a more upmarket seafood restaurant, Marinero El Templete.

**La Bodeguita del Medio $$**$ *Empredado, 207 e/ San Ignacio y Cuba, tel:* (7) 867 1374. Open daily noon–midnight. Now in its seventh decade, this scruffy, graffiti-scrawled den has played host to celebrities from Sinatra to Salvador Allende. Now a stream of tourists sips mojitos, but the food and service suffers.

**Café del Oriente $$$** *Plaza de San Francisco, tel:* (7) 860 6686. Open daily noon–midnight. This slick international restaurant in a beautiful colonial mansion is where to go for that dress-up, blow-out meal. Extensive wine list. Sit on the square for coffee or cocktails.

**Café Taberna Beny Moré $$** *Mercaderes 531 esq. a Teniente Rey (corner of Plaza Vieja), tel:* (7) 861 1637. Open daily noon–midnight. In what was Havana's oldest café, named after its first owner, Juan Batista de Taberna, it has been made over with a Beny Moré theme. Live bands day and night; the atmosphere is better than the food.

**La Divina Pastora $$–$$$** *Fortaleza de la Cabaña, tel:* (7) 860 8341. Open daily noon–11pm.* Take the tunnel under the harbour to reach this stylish restaurant, set in a beautifully converted old battery by the waterside below the fort. Great view of Havana skyline. Fish and seafood dishes and correct, swift service.

**Los Nardos $$$$** *Paseo de Martí 563, e/ Teniente Rey y Dragones, tel: (7) 863 2895.* Open daily noon–midnight. Quirky and popular, no reservations so wait in line. Decorated with soccer memorabilia and 1930s trophies. Huge portions of meat, fish and lobster. Upstairs with no queue are El Trofeo, serving Cuban and international food, or El Asturianito, for Cuban and Italian food, including good pizzas.

**Nerei $$** *Calle 19, 110, e/ L y M, Vedado, tel: (7) 832 7860.* Open daily noon–midnight. Good Cuban dishes served in a dining room stuffed with antiques or outside on the terrace surrounded by plants. Roast suckling pig *(lechón asado)* is the house speciality.

**Paladar La Julia $** *O'Reilly 506A, tel: (7) 862 7438.* Open daily noon–11pm. A traditional *paladar* offering huge portions of Cuban food, including good rice and beans. Popular, so come early or make a reservation.

**El Patio $$–$$$** *Plaza de la Catedral, tel: (7) 867 1034.* Open daily noon–midnight. One of the capital's romantic settings for a meal, in one of Havana's most splendidly painted and restored colonial courtyards. Creole fare is decent, but it can't match the surroundings. The popular drinks terrace looks out on the Plaza de la Catedral.

## CENTRO, VEDADO AND MIRAMAR

**1830 $$$** *Malecón 12502 e/. Av. 20 y 22, Vedado, tel: (7) 838 3090.* Open noon–midnight. A popular restaurant right at the mouth of the river, a great location for weddings and family celebrations. International food well prepared. Dinner is followed by a cabaret at 10pm and lots of live music.

**El Aljibe $$** *Av. 7 e/ 24 y 26, Miramar, tel: (7) 204 1583.* Open daily for lunch and dinner. One of the best dining experiences in the capital is at this thatched-roof restaurant out in Miramar, offering top-flight Creole cooking. The speciality is the all-you-can-eat lemony chicken (*pollo asado El Ajibe*), with salad, plantains, chips, rice and beans.

**La Guarida $$** *Calle Concordia, 418, e/ Gervasio y Escobar, Centro Habana, tel: (7) 866 9047, www.laguarida.com.* Open daily noon–midnight. The most famous *paladar* in Havana, in the crumbling building where much of the Cuban film *Fresa y* Chocolate was filmed. Creative, wonderfully prepared food.

**La Torre $$$** *M esq.17, Vedado, tel: (7) 832 7306.* Open daily noon–midnight. At the top of the FOCSA building with great views all over Havana. The restaurant has a high-class kitchen serving French and international food. Open for lunch and dinner, you can stay on till late for drinks at the bar.

## VIÑALES

**Casa de Don Tomás $–$$** *Salvador Cisneros 140.* Open for lunch and dinner. Completely rebuilt after a hurricane destroyed the former handsome colonial building dating from 1879. Food average but it is a pleasant place to come for live music and a cocktail.

## VARADERO

**Albacora $–$$** *Calle 59 e/. Av 1ra y Playa, tel: (45) 668 050.* Open daily 9am–midnight. Pleasant setting on a terrace overlooking the sea and a good place to come for seafood.

**Mansión Xanadú $$$** *Av. Las Américas, km 4.5, tel: (45) 667 750.* Open daily noon–10.30pm. Grand seaside mansion serving international dishes with variable success. Lunchtime snacks available on the terrace. On the third floor the Casa Blanca Panoramic Bar has cocktails and live music.

## CIENFUEGOS

**Palacio del Valle $$$** *Calle 37 esq. 2, Punta Gorda, tel: (43) 551 226.* Open daily 10am–11pm. Next to the Hotel Jagua, this ornate early

20th-century Moorish palace (see page 61) has a ground-floor restaurant serving reasonable seafood and paella. Rooftop bar.

## TRINIDAD

**Estela $–$$** *Calle Simón Bolívar, 557, tel: (41) 994 329.* Open Mon–Fri from 7pm, This *paladar* is probably the most popular place to eat so get there early. Tables are set in a walled garden among the shrubs. The food is fresh, imaginative and there is an extensive menu. Portions are generous and service is friendly.

**San José $–$$** *Maceo No. 382 entre Colon y Smith, tel: (41) 994 702.* A trendy *paladar* which probably serves the best pizza on the island. Another good option is the fried plantains stuffed with beef and cheese. Make sure to arrive before 6pm as it gets busy later on. Excellent value for money.

**Sol y Son $–$$** *Calle Simón Bolívar, 283, e/ Frank País y José Martí.* Open daily 7–11pm. A colonial house with an entryway that might be an antiques shop and peaceful courtyard, offering such dishes as *cerdo borracho* (drunken pork with rum) and stuffed fish.

## CAMAGÜEY

**1800 $$** *Plaza San Juan de Dios #113 entre San Rafael y San Juan de Dios; tel: (32) 283 619.* Situated on the city's most beautiful square, this lovely restaurant offers a good variety of tasty Cuban staples, seafood and tapas, plus an excellent buffet. Great atmosphere and music.

**Campana de Toledo $** *Plaza San Juan de Dios, tel: (32) 286 812.* Open daily for lunch and dinner. Good – if not memorable – Spanish and Creole fare in one of the city's prettiest courtyards. Live music. Busy at lunch with tour parties.

## GUARDALAVACA

**El Ancla $$** *Playa Guardalavaca, Banes, tel: (24) 430 381.* Open daily 9am–10.30pm. Seafood platters and pastas and a waterside cocktail terrace in a fabulous site at the eastern end of the beach (cross the beach and river to reach it). A lovely spot for a lobster lunch.

## SANTIAGO DE CUBA

**El Morro $$–$$$** *Carretera del Morro, tel: (22) 691 576*. Open daily noon–10pm. In a superb clifftop location on a vine-covered terrace next to Castillo del Morro, this restaurant offers excellent Creole fare including shrimp and lobster along with the coastal views.

**Santiago 1900 $–$$** *Bartolomé Masó, 354, e/ Hartmann y Pío Rosado, tel: (22) 623 507*. Open daily for lunch and dinner. This spectacular mansion has a beautiful courtyard and two terraces upstairs. You can pay in *pesos cubanos*, which makes a meal absurdly cheap. However, the *criollo* cooking is mostly hit or miss, as are the mojitos.

**Zunzún $$$** *Avenida Manduley 159 esq Calle 7, Vista Alegre, tel: (22) 641 528*. Daily noon–9pm. Elegant dining with marble floors and crystal chandeliers. The food is good, particularly the lobster, and the service is attentive.

## BARACOA

**La Colonial $** *José Martí 123, tel: (21) 645 391*. Open daily for dinner. Of Baracoa's many good *paladares*, this is one of the nicest, with a seductive decor and ambience, a pretty courtyard and such local fare as coconut-flavoured fish-and-rice dishes and sweet *cucurucho* (shredded coconut with fruit flavouring). Vegetarian options available. Good service.

# A–Z TRAVEL TIPS

A Summary of Practical Information

# A

## ACCOMMODATION

Standards and facilities have improved dramatically over the past few years. Cuba's new or restored hotels in beach resorts and in Havana typically have pools, restaurants, buffets, boutiques, air conditioning and satellite TV. Top resort hotels offer round-the-clock entertainment, while simpler resort hotels offer some in-house entertainment and invariably have a pool. Elsewhere, there are large, Soviet-style concrete eyesores located on the outskirts of towns, but there are now a number of small, attractive boutique hotels in town centres in renovated old hotels with plenty of character.

*Casas particulares* – private accommodation in Cuban homes – are inexpensive alternatives that allow foreigners a view of local life. Prices range from CUC$25–50 per double room in Havana and Santiago to CUC$15–25 in less-visited places; you may be able to bargain down the quoted price for long stays. Be cautious when looking for a *casa*. Avoid intermediaries if possible, and visit the room before committing yourself. Try to stay only at licensed *casas*. Owners of unlicensed *casas* risk ruinous fines if caught.

Outside such high periods as Christmas, New Year and Easter, you don't always need advance reservations, but it helps. Your host will often come to the bus station to pick you up so you don't get lost or diverted to another *casa*. For reservations from abroad it is worth checking www.casaparticularcuba.org.

I'd like a room with twin beds/double bed **Quisiera una habitación con dos camas/cama matrimonial**
What's the price? **¿Cuál es el precio?**
Is breakfast included? **¿El desayuno está incluído?**
Is there a private homestay near here? **¿Conoce una casa particular por aquí?**

## AIRPORTS (see Getting There)

Cuba's main airport is Havana's José Martí International Airport (tel: (7) 266 4133 (7) 649 5777; http://havana.airportcuba.net), located 20km (12 miles) south of downtown Havana. Hotel and long distance bus reservations can be made at the airport's Infotur office. Varadero's Juan Gualberto Gómez Airport is 22km (14 miles) west of Varadero. Santiago de Cuba's Antonio Maceo Airport is located 6km (4 miles) south of that city. There are also international airports in Camagüey, Cayo Coco, Cayo Largo, Ciego de Avila, Holguín, Santa Clara, Las Tunas and Manzanillo.

On arrival, if you're on a package holiday a bus will transfer you to your hotel. Independent travellers can book transfers through agencies in their own country; otherwise take a taxi or a bus from Terminal 1 (the domestic flights terminal); buses run until 8pm and payment is by CUPs. From the airport, it costs CUC$25 to downtown Havana (usually less to return); CUC$10–15 to the centre of Santiago). It's a 40-minute trip from José Martí airport to central Havana. You must pay a departure tax at all airports: CUC$25.

## B

## BICYCLE HIRE

With the scarcity of public transport, millions of Cubans ride bikes. Most resorts have bikes and mopeds to hire. Many rental bikes are old and have few gears, and serious cyclists intending to tour the country should bring their bikes, as well as plenty of parts and spare tubes. Alternatively, you could try a bike tour with a Canadian-based company WoWCuba (www.wowcuba.com), which also has a branch in Havana.

## BUDGETING FOR YOUR TRIP

Compared with the rest of Latin America and other developing countries, Cuba can be surprisingly expensive, but it compares well with the rest of the Caribbean.

**Transport to Cuba.** The airfare is likely to be your greatest expenditure, especially if coming from Europe or Asia. It's cheapest to travel outside of high season (mid-Dec to mid-Apr) or on a package tour.

**Accommodation.** Hotels in Havana, Santiago and major resorts are expensive, comparable to North America and Europe. In resorts, all-inclusive deals (meals, drinks and entertainment) can be a good option. Private houses *(casas particulares)* are generally inexpensive.

**Meals and drinks.** State-owned restaurants range from moderate to expensive. Lobster and other shellfish are the most expensive items. *Paladares* (private restaurants in Cuban homes) or homecooked meals in *casas particulares* are inexpensive alternatives. Alcohol and beer are considerably cheaper than in the UK, and slightly cheaper than in the rest of Europe.

**Local transport.** Urban public transport is cheap and improving but still crowded and inefficient. Taxis and *bicitaxis* are the best way to get about within cities and resorts; they are inexpensive.

**Incidentals.** Entertainment in cabarets and discos is expensive for Cuba (CUC$10–90), and drinks in such nightspots are also much more expensive than in bars and cafés. Gifts like prestigious hand-rolled cigars are expensive, even if much cheaper than they are abroad.

## C

## CAMPING

There are official campsites in isolated locations all over the island, but they offer basic huts rather than tents. In each major town ask for the Campismo office for local campsites, most of which are used by Cubans on holiday. There are also 21 campsites, hotels or parking sites for tourists using camper vans, with water, power and waste disposal, dotted around the island. Book through an agency abroad, which will issue a voucher for you to present to Campertour (Calle 3 y Malecón, Vedado).

## CAR HIRE

There are good reasons for not hiring a car in Cuba. It can be expensive, petrol (gasoline) is pricey by North American standards (although not when compared to the UK), and rental firms are often inefficient and difficult to deal with in the event of car damage or other problems. If you wish to hire a car in one place and return it in another, you must pay the cost of having it returned to its origin. Long-distance buses are reliable and, along with tour buses, go to most places of interest, but only a hire car will allow you to go anywhere you wish, when you wish. To hire a car, you must be at least 21 and have had a year's driving experience. You will need a national or international licence.

Cuba has none of the major international rental agencies. However, there are good local hire firms with offices throughout the island. Here are the main ones: Vía Rentacar (www.carrentalcuba.com), Havanautos (www.havanautos.cu), Cubacar (www.transtur.cu) and Rex (www.rexcarrental.com). Rates range from CUC$45 to $100 per day for unlimited mileage. Insurance must be paid locally even if you have prepaid the car hire abroad. If there is any damage to the car, you must pay the first few hundred dollars-worth of repair unless you prove the accident wasn't your fault. You must leave a cash or open credit-card guarantee to cover for this eventuality. Inspect the car before you set off to identify existing dents and scratches.

> I'd like to rent a car for a day/a week **Quisiera alquilar un auto/carro por un día/una semana**
> Fill it up. **Llénelo, por favor.**

## CLIMATE

Cuba has a subtropical climate: hot and humid. The chart below shows the average daily temperature in Havana. For beach lovers and sightseers, November to May is the ideal time to visit, though there is plenty of sunshine year-round. Hurricane season lasts from June until the end of November. The more active should avoid the height of summer, when it's debilitatingly hot and wet. The mountains are cooler and the south and east drier and warmer. Oriente, the area around Santiago, can be wickedly hot–much hotter than the western region.

| | J | F | M | A | M | J | J | A | S | O | N | D |
|---|---|---|---|---|---|---|---|---|---|---|---|---|
| °C | 22 | 22 | 23 | 25 | 26 | 27 | 28 | 28 | 27 | 26 | 24 | 22 |
| °F | 72 | 72 | 73 | 77 | 79 | 81 | 82 | 82 | 81 | 79 | 75 | 72 |

## CLOTHING

During the day you'll rarely need more than shorts or a skirt and a T-shirt (and swimsuit). At night in winter, a light sweater or jacket may be needed. In upmarket hotels, restaurants and nightclubs you are required to dress equally smartly.

## CRIME AND SAFETY (see also Emergencies and Police)

Cuba is a remarkably safe place in which to travel – one of the safest anywhere. The crime that does exist is generally directed at possessions rather than people, so place temptation out of sight. Most top hotels provide safes, though usually with a rental charge.

City streets at night feel more dangerous than they actually are because they are so poorly lit. The one area where you should be wary of purse-snatchers is in Old Havana, particularly on Calle Obispo and the grid of streets south of it to the train station. Central Havana west of the Prado to the Hotel Deauville also has a bad reputation.

I want to report a theft. **Quiero denunciar un robo.**
my wallet/handbag/passport **mi cartera/bolso/pasaporte**
my camera **mi cámara**
safe (deposit box) **caja fuerte**

# D

## DRIVING

**Road conditions.** There is little traffic outside of town centres. Most main roads are paved and in fairly good condition, although they are not well signposted. The Autopista Nacional (motorway) runs from Havana west to Pinar del Río and east to Jatibonico, just before Ciego de Avila. From there a good road heads east to Santiago de Cuba. A number of rural roads are not paved. Beware of potholes: some are big enough to cause real damage. Other hazards are cyclists, hidden railway crossings and wandering livestock. Driving at night is not advisable.

**Rules and regulations.** To drive, you must be 21 and have a valid driver's licence. Drive on the right. Speed limits, strictly enforced, are 100km/h (62mph) on the highway (motorway), 90km/h (56mph) on other open roads, 60km/h (37mph) on smaller rural roads and 40km/h (25mph) in urban areas. You are likely to get an on-the-spot fine if caught breaking the speed limit. Insurance is mandatory, as is wearing seatbelts. It's common practice to sound your horn when passing to let vehicles without rearview mirrors know what's happening.

**Fuel** (*gasolina*). Cupet stations are spread throughout the country and are open 24 hours. They are not self service. Petrol or diesel must be paid for in CUC$. The quality of regular petrol is poor, and many rental companies insist that you purchase expensive '*especial*' fuel.

stop **pare**
caution **cuidado**
no parking **no parqueo**
give way (yield) **ceda el paso**
one-way **dirección única**

danger **peligro**
car registration papers **permiso de circulación**
driver's licence **licencia de manejar**
How do I get to … ? **¿Cómo se puede ir a … ?**
Is this the right street for … ? **¿Es ésta la calle que va a … ?**
Full tank, please. **Llénelo, por favor.**
My car has broken down. **Mi carro tiene problemas mecánicos.**
I have a flat tire. **Tengo la goma ponchada.**
May I park here? **¿Se puede aparcar aquí?**
Is this the highway (road) to … ? **¿Es ésta la carretera hacia … ?**

## E

## ELECTRICITY

Electrical appliances in hotels and *casas particulares* operate on either 110 volts or 220 volts. Most outlets accept flat-pin plugs, some round-pin plugs. Take an adapter; a converter might also be necessary.

What's the voltage? **¿Cuál es el voltaje?**
adaptor/a battery **un adaptador/una pila**

## EMBASSIES

**Canada:** Calle 30, no. 518, e/ 5 y 7, Miramar, Havana, tel: (7) 204 2516, (7) 204 7079; www.canadainternational.gc.ca.
**UK:** Calle 34, no. 702/4, esq 7, Miramar, Havana, tel: (7) 214 2200. The UK embassy also represents New Zealand interests and will help Australian and Irish citizens in an emergency.
**US:** The US has an Interests Section (in Swiss embassy): Calzada e/ L y M, Vedado, Havana, tel: (7) 839 4101-0. For travellers, this office acts in the same way as an American embassy.

## EMERGENCIES (see also Health and Medical Care and Police)

Asistur, a state-run organisation, helps foreigners with medical or financial problems and is affiliated with a number of international travel insurance companies. For a 10 percent commission, they can negotiate a cash advance if provided with bank details overseas. They can also help to find lost luggage and issue travel documents. Asistur's main office is at Paseo del Prado, 208 e/ Colón y Trocadero, Old Havana, tel: (7) 866 4499, www.asistur.cu. There are also offices in Cayo Coco, Guardalavaca, Santiago and Varadero. All offices open 24 hours.
**Useful telephone numbers:** Police 106, Fire 105, Ambulance 104, Information 113. These numbers may not work in remote areas so ask your hotel or *casa particular* or call Asistur, where you will be put through to someone who speaks English.

# G

## GAY AND LESBIAN TRAVELLERS

Cuba is not as virulently anti-gay as are many parts of Catholic Latin America. In fact, since the 1980s Cuban society has become considerably more tolerant and inclusive. Still, discrimination and harassment exist, though they are unlikely to affect most gay travellers. *Jineteros* (male prostitutes) targeting gays are common. Areas known to be popular include the Malecón, the bars in Old Havana, and the bars and restaurants around the Coppelia ice cream park in Vedado. Humboldt 52 (Humboldt #52 esq. Infanta y Hospital) is advertised as the "first full-time openly-gay bar". Other gay friendly venues include Cabaret Las Vegas, Cine Club Diferente and Fashion Bar Havana.

## GETTING THERE (see also Airports)

Most flights into Cuba are charters, arriving at Havana, Varadero and several other airports convenient to beach resorts such as Cayo Coco, Playa Santa Lucía and Guardalavaca. From Canada, scheduled flights to Cuba leave from Montreal or Toronto, taking around four hours.

There are also charters from Vancouver, Halifax and Ottawa. From Europe, Cubana flies from London, Paris, Moscow, Madrid and Rome; Air France flies to Havana from Paris; Iberia flies from Madrid and Virgin Atlantic flies from London. From Australia and New Zealand, the options include travelling through Canada, Mexico or other points in Latin America.

For those travelling legally to Cuba, regular flights to Havana from the US originate in Los Angeles, Miami and New York. If you have authorisation to travel to Cuba, contact Marazul Tours (tel: 800-223 5334; www.marazul.com).

Those wishing to circumvent travel restrictions from the US usually go through Canada (Toronto, Montreal, Vancouver), Mexico (Mexico City, Mérida, Cancún), Bahamas (Nassau) or Jamaica (Kingston, Montego Bay). Havanatur, www.havanatur.com is an online travel service which handles tourist cards as well as roundtrip air tickets on Cubana Aviación.

Similar arrangements can be made through Canadian, Jamaican and Mexican airlines and travel agencies.

## GUIDES AND TOURS

Most still come to Cuba on package tours, which may include a group excursion or two. If you wish to travel independently and have found a hotel-airfare package that is cheaper than separate arrangements or airfare alone, you are not obligated to go along with the group once in Cuba. Plenty of people check into their resort hotels and take off on their own.

The most popular and straightforward way of exploring Cuba is on group excursions. However, these trips–available in any tourist hotel and led by English-speaking tour guides–may insulate you from the most interesting aspects of Cuban life. You can reach virtually the whole island from any resort on excursions; most are flexible and will allow you to break up a daytrip and stay overnight if you wish to explore on your own.

Freelance 'guides', offering to take you to *casas particulares* and *pala-*

*dares* (privately run lodgings and restaurants) or obtain cigars and prostitutes, are omnipresent in Cuba.

Another way to explore the island, albeit a more expensive one, is on a Harley Davidson with La Poderosa Tours (www.lapoderosatours. com), run by the son of Che Guevara. Prices for a six day tour start from US$3000.

## H

## HEALTH AND MEDICAL CARE (see also Emergencies)

Cuba's national health system has made it one of the healthiest countries in the developing world. There are no mandatory vaccinations required for travel to Cuba; nonetheless, some health professionals recommend vaccinations against typhoid and hepatitis A.

Although Cuban water is chlorinated, tap water is not generally safe to drink. Bottled mineral water (*agua mineral*) is widely available and recommended. The most likely source of food poisoning is from unhygienic hotel buffet food. Cuban food is very plain, and upset stomachs are less common than in many other countries.

The Cuban sun can burn fair-skinned people within minutes. Use plenty of sunscreen and wear a hat. It's also easy to become dehydrated, so be sure to drink plenty of water. Mosquitoes are a menace from dusk to dawn in coastal resorts. Air conditioning helps keep them at bay, but apply insect repellent.

If you need to see a doctor, contact your hotel's reception desk. Large resort hotels have their own doctor. All the island's main resorts have an international clinic (*clínica internacional*), as do Havana, Santiago de

I'm sick. **Estoy enfermo(a)**.
Where's the nearest hospital?**¿Dónde está el hospital más cercano?**
Call a doctor/dentist. **Llame a un médico/dentista.**

Cuba, Cienfuegos and Trinidad. Medical treatment in Cuba is excellent and free for Cubans. Foreigners, however, must pay. Such treatment is expensive, so proper insurance is essential; it is mandatory to have health insurance before you arrive in Cuba.

Every town has an all-night pharmacy *(farmacia)*. The range of medicines has become severely limited. Resorts have better-stocked international pharmacies, though prices can be astronomical.

## HITCH-HIKING

Although hitching a ride in Cuba is easy and safe, it is not recommended because of the possibility that police may fine your benefactor on suspicion that he's earning dollars illegally. If you're looking to hitch, the biggest problem you'll encounter is the paucity of vehicles (at least outside the major cities).

## L

## LANGUAGE

The official language is Spanish, Increasing numbers of Cubans are learning English (French, Italian and other languages), and many people in the tourist industry are fluent, but you will most likely need some Spanish, especially outside tourist hotels and major resorts. The *Berlitz Latin American Spanish Phrase Book & Dictionary* includes over 1,200 phrases useful for travellers.

## M

## MAPS

The best road map of Cuba is 'Guía de Carreteras' by the Directorio Turístico de Cuba (on sale in Cuba for CUC$12). Other maps are 'Cuba: ITM 190' (ITMB), 'Cuba' (Globetrotter Travel Map) and 'Cuba' (Nelles Map). Hotels and bookshops in Havana and Santiago sell reasonable maps and the Infotur desk at Havana airport is a good place to look on arrival.

## MEDIA

You will not receive much outside news in Cuba, although many tourist hotels offer CNN. You might find a stray European newpaper at major hotels in Havana or resorts, but it's not likely. The main national newspaper, *Granma*, is the mouthpiece of the government. A weekly *Granma* international edition is published in English, French and German, with cultural features of tourist appeal. Other national newspapers include the weekly *Trabajadores* ('Workers') and *Juventud Rebelde* ('Rebel Youth'). *Bohemia*, a respected biweekly magazine founded in 1908, has in-depth analysis of contemporary Cuba and the world as seen through Cuban eyes.

Radio Taíno (1160 AM), a tourist-oriented music station with some broadcasts in English, is most easily heard around Havana. Tune in to the American Forces Network around Guantánamo on 102.1 FM and 103.1 FM for insights into life in the US naval base.

Of the five state-run television channels, one, Cubavision International, can only be seen on cable TV and is on air 24 hours a day.

## MONEY

**Currency.** Cuba has two currencies, the *peso cubano* (CUP), or national peso, and the *peso convertible* (CUC), or convertible peso. The latter is the one which tourists use most of the time, as it is fully exchangeable for foreign currencies. Tourists have to use the *peso convertible* for all payments such as restaurant bills, hotel bills (if not paid in advance), transport and souvenirs. The only time *pesos cubanos* are needed is in very out of the way places, for street food, snacks or in a rural market, or if you take a local bus. Local town buses cost 20–40 centavos and you are unlikely to need to exchange more than US$5 into *pesos cubanos* for a two-week stay. Spend all your CUCs before you leave the island, as they can't be exchanged outside Cuba. The only place in Cuba where you can change pesos into other currencies is at Havana airport.

**Currency exchange.** For accounting purposes, the *peso convertible* is fixed at US$1 = CUC$1, but there is a 10 percent tax on all US

> Do you accept traveller's cheques? **¿Cheques de viajero?**
> May I pay with a credit card? **¿Se puede pagar con tarjeta?**
> How much is that? **¿Cuánto es?**

dollar exchange transactions. You are advised to bring euros, sterling or Canadian dollars, which do not attract the tax. Bring plenty of cash and make sure that the notes are clean and undamaged; any with writing on them or tears will be rejected. There are banks and *casas de cambio* (exchange houses, called a CADECA) where you can exchange your money. There is no black market. If you want to buy *pesos cubanos*, the rate is CUC$1 = CUP26.

**Credit cards** (*tarjetas de crédito*). An increasing number of outlets accept credit cards, including many tourist shops, upmarket hotels and restaurants, airlines, petrol stations and car hire companies. Following the restoration of US-Cuban diplomatic relations in 2014, MasterCard started accepting US-issued credit cards. Other major credit card operators including American Express and Visa are set to follow suit. Nevertheless, nobody should rely solely on credit cards, as not everybody accepts them and, even if they do, telephone lines are sometimes out of action so payments cannot be processed. Cuba remains a largely cash (*divisa*) economy.

**Traveller's cheques** (*cheques de viajero*). Traveller's cheques in dollars are accepted (in places that usually also accept credit cards), but they must not currently be American Express or others drawn on US banks. The easiest way to change traveller's cheques into pesos is at hotels; at a bank or CADECA, you'll need your passport and the official receipt from the cheque-issuing institution. Commission rates are 2–4 percent. If you've mistakenly arrived in Cuba with American Express traveller's cheques, Asistur (see page 119) can cash them for a 10 percent commission.

**ATMs.** Cuba has a growing network of automatic teller machines in cities. Your hotel will know if ATMs are in place by the time of your trip. Several banks (Banco Financiero is one) and CADECAs give over-the-counter cash advances on credit or debit cards on production of a passport, but charge high commission.

## O

## OPENING HOURS

Offices are usually open weekdays from 8am to 5pm, with a one-hour lunch break. Some are open on Saturday mornings, from 8am to noon or 1pm. Banks are typically open weekdays from 8.30am to 3pm.

Some museums open daily, but most close for one day (usually Monday) and also close on Sunday at noon or 1pm. Typical museum hours are 9am (sometimes 8am or 10am) until 5pm (sometimes 4pm or 6pm). Regardless of when you go, you'll find several closed for renovations; make inquiries before travelling a long way.

Restaurants do not typically stay open late; most close their doors around 10pm or even earlier. The great exception is *paladares*, which are usually open from noon to 11pm or midnight.

## P

## POLICE

Most police are helpful and friendly, even though they occasionally harass Cubans (or, more specifically, anyone of dark skin colour who might be assumed to be Cuban) accompanying foreigners. If you are robbed, make sure you get a police report, a time-consuming affair.

## POST OFFICES

You can buy stamps *(sellos)* with *pesos* convertibles at hotels, although this costs more than if you buy them with *pesos cubanos* at post offices. Some stamps are not sticky and you have to ask a post office or hotel desk for glue. Cuba's post system is unreliable and slow. Postcards *(tarjetas postales)* sent to Europe take from two weeks to a month or more to arrive.

Post offices are generally open weekdays 8am to 5pm and Saturday

9am to 3pm. You'll find post offices in every rural town; cities have several branches. In Havana, the best one to use is the one in the Hotel Havana Libre in Vedado (Calles L and 23). More efficient mailing services are available through DHL Worldwide Express, with offices in several cities. In Havana, there's one in the Hotel Havana Libre.

## PUBLIC HOLIDAYS

The following days are public holidays in Cuba:

**1 January** Anniversary of the Triumph of the Revolution: Liberation Day

**19 April** Anniversary of the Bay of Pigs victory

**1 May** International Workers' Day (Labour Day)

**25–27 July** National Rebellion Day (26 July)

**10 October** Independence Day

## R

## RELIGION

Roman Catholicism in Cuba is strongly intertwined with Afro-Cuban religions such as *santería* (see page 33). Many aspects of these religious practices can be experienced by visitors. The government blunted the power and influence of the Catholic Church in the early 1960s, but mass is still said in churches throughout the island, and since the Pope's visits to Cuba in 1998 and 2012 there has been a resurgence of Catholic practice.

## T

## TELEPHONES

Cuba's country code is 53. In addition, each area of the island has its own area code (for Havana it is 7). To make an international call from Cuba dial 119, then the country code, the area code and the phone number. To make a domestic call, add the area code (for example, 7 for Havana).

For interprovincial calls you first have to dial the appropriate prefix (0 to and from Havana, 01 for all other provinces), followed by the area code, then the number itself. When phoning Cuba from abroad, drop the 0 or 01. Dial 113 for the free domestic telephone enquiries service.

Top hotels have direct-dial facilities for all calls. Elsewhere you can make domestic calls on a direct line, but you will need to go through the hotel operator for international calls. International calls from Cuba are very expensive (CUC$2.20–4.40 per minute). As they do everywhere in the world, hotels charge a significant surcharge on calls.

Public phones which take coins (20 centavos or 1 peso Cubano) are now rare; most have been converted to take pre-paid phone cards (tarjetas). Tourists are supposed to buy them in CUC$, in denominations of CUC$10–50, while Cubans pay in CUP$. The state telecommunications company is ETECSA, also known as Telepunto, which offers a full range of services.

Mobile phones can be rented through Cubacel, which can be found at ETECSA and Telepunto offices. They cost about CUC$5 a day to hire and call charges are high. You can use your own phone in Cuba (where there is a signal) and texting is often cheaper, quicker and easier than queuing to use the internet at ETECSA. All mobile numbers begin with 5 and have 8 digits. To call a mobile from Havana dial 0 and then the number, from other provinces dial 01 and then the number. Area codes are not needed.

I'd like make a telephone call ... **Quisiera hacer una llamada ...**

to England/Canada/ United States. **a Inglaterra/Canadá/los Estados Unidos.**

reverse-charge call **cobro revertido**

Can you get me this number in ... ? **¿Puede comunicarme con este número en ... ?**

phone card **tarjeta telefónica**

## TIME ZONES

Cuba is five hours behind GMT. It operates on Eastern Standard Time in winter and Daylight Saving Time (one hour later) from April to October.

| San Francisco | Cuba | New York | London | Sydney |
|---|---|---|---|---|
| 9am | noon | noon | 5pm | 2am |

## TIPPING

In restaurants tip CUC$1–2 per person, or 10 percent. In bars, loose (*peso convertible*) change is acceptable. Tour guides expect at least CUC$2 for their services, and roving musical groups should be given a peso convertible.

## TOILETS

It's often best to carry a roll of toilet paper with you at all times in Cuba, as many establishments do not provide their own. Those that do often demand a few cents for providing it – so it's worth carrying some small change.

## TOURIST INFORMATION

There are official Cuban government tourism offices in Canada and Britain but not in the US:
**Canada:** 1200 Bay Street, Suite 305, Toronto, Ontario M5R 2A5, tel: (416) 362 0700; www.gocuba.ca.
**UK:** 154 Shaftesbury Avenue, London WC2H 8HL, tel: (020) 7240 6655; www.travel2cuba.co.uk.
In Cuba itself, there is no centralised system providing tourism information, and reliable information is sometimes hard to come by. Instead, you must rely upon hotels and travel agencies, whose primary function is to sell excursion packages. In Cuba all hotels have a tourism desk (*buró de turismo*).

Infotur is the only tourist information service, although other state tour operators will help. The main office is at Obispo, 521 e/ Bernaza y Villegas in Old Havana, tel: (7) 866 3333. Other branches are at the airport terminals; Av. Las Terrazas e/ 11 y 12, Santa María del Mar, Playas del Este, tel: (7) 797 1261; Av. 5 y 112, Miramar, tel: (7) 204 7036; and Obispo y San Ignacio, Old Havana, tel: (7) 863 6884.

## TRANSPORT

**Taxis.** There is only one state taxi company, Cubataxi, tel: (7) 796 6666 in Havana. You can call them or pick them up from designated ranks (usually outside hotels, major museums, bus stations and airports). They are metered and fares are paid in *pesos convertibles*. Private taxis (which might or might not be licensed) also circulate. The lumbering vintage American cars with taxi signs (*colectivos* or *máquinas*) have fixed routes and are usually reserved for Cubans, although the smarter versions, owned by the Grancar company, are state-owned and geared towards tourists – in Havana call (7) 338 417980.

You can hire any taxi for a single fare or a day. Many owners of private cars *(particulares)* also operate legally as freelance taxi drivers, although it is illegal for them to carry tourists. Owners face large fines if caught, so it's best to ride in official taxis.

**Buses** (*guaguas*, pronounced 'wah-wahs'). Buses are the backbone of Cuba's public transport system, but urban buses in Havana are not a great option for tourists. There are too few of them, they're uncomfortable, they're usually full when they do arrive, there are long queues and there is a risk of being pickpocketed. A better option for tourists is the hop-on, hop-off service called the HabanaBusTour, CUC$5 per day, with three routes, one from the Parque Central to Vedado, another out to Playas del Este via the Castillo del Morro, and a third one to Marina Hemingway. A similar service operates in Varadero all along the peninsula as far as Matanzas.

For travel between cities, towns and resorts of major tourist interest, however, there is a company named Víazul (Av. 26 e/ Av. Zoológico y

Ulloa, Nuevo Vedado; tel: (7) 881 1413, 883 6092; www.viazul.com).
It operates air-conditioned tour buses to Varadero, Viñales/Pinar del
Río, Cienfuegos, Trinidad, Santa Clara, Sancti Spíritus, Ciego de Ávila,
Camagüey, Holguín, Las Tunas, Bayamo and Santiago de Cuba. Prices
range from US$10 (Havana to Varadero Airport) to US$51 (Havana to
Santiago). If you're not hiring a car in Cuba but travelling independently, Víazul is the way to go. It's far more efficient, faster and more
reliable than trains. Another company, Astro, also runs long-distance
buses but they are for Cubans.

**Trains** (*trenes*). Journeys are extremely slow, schedules unreliable, and
breakdowns are frequent. There are no express trains, almost all are
local services that stop at every station. Trains usually run only on alternate days or a couple of times a week to most destinations. The train
between Havana and Santiago de Cuba takes at least 15 hours, usually
many more. It runs every other day, with stops at Santa Clara, Camagüey and Santiago (CUC$50, cash only). In Havana you can make
bookings at the Estación Central, Arsenal y Ejido (tel: (7) 861 1920).

**Domestic flights.** Flying in Cuba is the quickest and most reliable form
of transport for long trips. It's also good value (flights range from about
CUC$43–143 each way). Flights fill up fast, so book in advance from
your home country if possible. Cubana, the national airline, provides domestic flights to 11 destinations from the capital, including to Baracoa,
Camagüey, Ciego de Ávila, Cienfuegos, Guantánamo, Holguín, Nueva
Gerona (Isla de la Juventud), Santiago and Varadero. Frequency varies
enormously, from several daily flights to Santiago to twice weekly to Baracoa. Tickets can be purchased in Cubana offices around the country
or from the main office in Havana on Calle 23 (La Rampa), no. 64 esq.
Infanta (tel: (7) 834 4446), or at the airport, Terminal 3 (tel: (7) 649 0410).

**Bicycle taxis** Havana's *cocotaxis* are yellow three-wheeled buggies
powered by motorcycle engines. They are just as plentiful as car taxis
in Havana and cost 50 centavos per kilometre. *Bicitaxis*, pedicabs, are a
fun way to traverse the city on short trips. Note that only some *bicitaxis* are licensed to carry foreigners; unlicensed ones should not be used.

**Horse carts** *(coches)*. Due to fuel shortages, in virtually every city except Havana and Santiago there are horses pulling covered carts and plush little carriages up and down the main streets. Ironically, horse carriages acting as taxis have become a tourist attraction in the resorts.

> When's the next bus/train to…? **¿Cuándo sale el próximo autobús/tren para…?**
> What's the fare to…? **¿Cuánto es la tarifa a…?**
> A ticket to… **Un billete para…**
> single (one-way) **ida**
> return (roundtrip) **ida y vuelta**

## VISAS AND ENTRY REQUIREMENTS

All visitors need a passport *(pasaporte)* that expires more than six months after your scheduled departure from Cuba and a return ticket. Tourists also need a tourist card *(tarjeta de turista)* to visit Cuba and health insurance valid for the duration of their stay. If you're travelling on a package holiday, the tour operator will arrange your tourist card for you. If travelling independently, contact your country's Cuban embassy; tourist cards (US$20–35 depending on the country) are also available from airline and travel agencies. The card is valid for 30 days. If you want to stay longer once in the country, you have to pay an additional fee and go, in person, to the Havana Immigration Office, Factor y Final, Nuevo Vedado, open 8.30am–noon. Business travellers require an official business visa from the nearest Cuban consulate, which can take several weeks; a letter of invitation is usually required.

The US trade embargo does not permit American citizens to spend money in Cuba without special permission. There are general and specific licences for government officials, representatives of international organisations, members of educational or cultural institutions, Cuban-Americans, journalists, religious or aid workers, researchers and athletes. Those covered by a general licence need no application or permission. Those wishing to travel officially with a specific licence should seek permission from the Licensing Division, Office of Foreign Assets Control (1500 Pennsylvania Avenue NW, Washington, D.C. 20220, tel: 202-622 2480) before contacting the Cuban Interests Section in Washington, D.C., for a visa.

*Any US citizen who travels to Cuba without authorisation by entering through a third country does so illegally.* Fines are established at up to US$250,000. Upon your return you might be harassed and have Cuban purchases confiscated. You might also be taken to court, so it is best to cover your tracks. However, Cuba welcomes American visitors. Cuban immigration officials do not stamp passports; they stamp only your tourist card instead. It should be noted, however, that due to the normalisation of relations between Cuba and US, the above-mentioned restrictions may soon be eased or lifted.

# W

## WEBSITES

Although few Cubans have access to the internet, Cuba is surprisingly well served by the web. From sites about the US embargo and travel restrictions to traveller recommendations, there is a wealth of information. A few sites worth exploring include the following:

www.dtcuba.com Cuban Tourist Directory site
www.cubaweb.cu Official government site
www.cubatravel.cu Official tourist site
www.cuba.com English/Spanish website packed with information
www.cubaabsolutely.com Spanish/English site with lots of information about Cuba and its culture
www.cuba-junky.com A comprehensive site for all Cuba lovers.
www.casaparticularcuba.org Accommodation booking service
www.lahabana.com A guide to the city and its arts and culture

## Recommended Hotels

The very best hotels are joint ventures with private firms from Spain, Canada and other countries. These are of an international standard. Many others, though, are a notch or two down from what you'd expect in Europe, North America or Asia. In Old Havana hotels in renovated colonial mansions are run by Habaguanex (www.habaguanexhotels. com) and are beautiful places to stay. At the inexpensive level, hotels around the island are often lacking in ambience and amenities.

*Casas particulares* – accommodation in private homes – are not only a better-quality and much cheaper alternative to the inexpensive hotels; they allow you a glimpse into unguarded Cuban life. They generally cost CUC$15–35 per room, depending on the location and the season. Your hosts usually also offer breakfast and evening meals at a small extra cost. You'll find a very abbreviated list of recommended private-home *casas* following the regular hotel listings below; however, others are very easy to find.

The price categories below, in US dollars, are for a standard double room, excluding meals, in high season (mid December to mid-April, July to August). Prices drop by 15–30 percent during other months. All accommodation is paid for in *pesos convertibles*. Only top hotels accept credit cards. For reservations it's best to call directly and get a confirmation number.

|  |  |
|---|---|
| $$$$ | over $150 |
| $$$ | $100–150 |
| $$ | $50–100 |
| $ | under $50 |

## HAVANA

## OLD HAVANA

**Ambos Mundos $–$$$** *Obispo 153 esq. Mercaderes, Habana Vieja, tel: (7) 860 9530, www.hotelambosmundos-cuba.com.* Hemingway wrote much of *For Whom the Bell Tolls* in room 511 of this historic hotel (opened in 1920). It's in the heart of Old Havana, on one of its most picturesque streets. The rooms are adequate in size, nicely decorated, but not all have windows to the outside. On the ground floor is an airy, lovely piano bar and the rooftop bar offers great views. 52 rooms.

**Hotel Florida $–$$**$ *Calle Obispo 252 esq. Cuba, Habana Vieja, tel: (7) 862 4127,* www.hotelfloridahavana.com. A marvellous colonial mansion built in 1836, achieves affordable luxury. It originally became a hotel in 1885 but reopened only in 1999. It is elegant, with plush public rooms, a lovely courtyard, and a great location just a couple of blocks from the Plaza de Armas. Some rooms have balconies. Piano bar, lobby bar and restaurant. 25 rooms.

**Hotel Mercure Sevilla $$$** *Trocadero, 55 e/ Zulueta y Animas, Habana Vieja, tel: (7) 860 8560,* www.accorhotels.com. This restored turn-of-the-20th-century establishment, of Spanish and Moroccan inspiration has a sumptuous lobby, magnificent rooftop restaurant and other excellent dining options. Guests have included Al Capone, Josephine Baker and Enrico Caruso, and scenes from Greene's *Our Man in Havana* were set here. Rooms are comfortable and stylish. Good pool, gymnasium, billiards/snooker, sauna, massage and solarium. 178 rooms.

**Hotel Santa Isabel $$$–$$$$** *Calle Baratillo, 9 e/ Obispo y Narciso López, Habana Vieja, tel: (7) 860 8201,* www.habaguanexhotels.com. This small, quiet, gorgeously restored hotel is an 18th-century palace right on the Plaza de Armas. Sumptuous rooms have period furniture, and the hotel features a lovely courtyard and great views from the roof. Recent guests have included former US President Jimmy Carter, Sting and Jack Nicholson. Breakfast is served overlooking the Plaza. 27 rooms and suites.

**Hostal Valencia $–$$** *Oficios, 53 esq. Obrapía, Habana Vieja, tel: (7) 867 1037,* www.habaguanexhotels.com. In an 18th-century mansion between Plaza de Armas and Plaza Vieja, this small Spanish-style yellow colonial is utterly charming. One of the city's best deals, it features rooms (no air conditioning) surrounding a delightful green courtyard. The Spanish restaurant is not so good. Book well in advance. 12 rooms.

## VEDADO

**Hotel Nacional de Cuba $$–$$$$** *Calle O esq. 21, Vedado, tel: (7) 836 3564,* www.hotelnacionaldecuba.com. A classic feature of New Havana, this landmark 1930 hotel rises above the Malecón. Former guests include Hemingway, Churchill, Frank Sinatra, Ava Gardner, Errol Flynn, Marlon Brando and gangsters Meyer Lansky and Lucky Luciano. Rooms are large, and most have sea views. It has a stunning dining room, two pools, a nightly cabaret show, gardens, terraces and bars. Prices include breakfast. 467 rooms.

**Tryp Habana Libre $$–$$$** *Calle L e/. 23 y 25, tel: (7) 834 6100,* www.meliacuba.com. An iconic tower hotel which opened in 1958 as the Hilton but was renamed in 1959 when it became the Revolutionary headquarters for a few months. Fascinating photos of that time line the hotel lobby. It is now a luxury hotel with lots of facilities including a shopping mall, airline offices, coffee shop, good restaurants and the Cabaret Turquino on the 25th floor with a roof which opens so you can dance under the stars. 569 rooms.

## PINAR DEL RÍO PROVINCE

**Horizontes La Ermita $–$$** *Carretera de la Ermita, km 2, Viñales, tel: (48) 796 250,* www.hotelescubanacan.com. This contemporary, low-slung hotel of Spanish colonial design is lacking in service and is simply and minimally furnished, but it has some of the finest views in the country, particularly from the swimming pool. All rooms open onto private balconies with chairs. The verdant valley and spectacular sunsets fill the horizon. An enjoyable 20-minute walk from Viñales town. 62 rooms.

**Horizontes Los Jazmines $–$$** *Carretera de Viñales, km 23.5 (3km from Viñales), tel: (48) 796 205,* www.hotelescubanacan.com. This pretty hotel on the edge of the beautiful Viñales valley has stupendous panoramic views. Bedrooms with balconies (in need of repair and redecoration), but with noisy air conditioning. The pool gets crowded, the food is mediocre. Horse-riding is available, and there are organised tours. 62 rooms and 16 small *cabañas.*

## ISLA DE LA JUVENTUD

**El Colony $$** *Carretera de Sigueanea, km 16, tel: (46) 398 181;* www.
hotelelcolony.com. On the coast, 42km (26 miles) southwest of
Nueva Gerona, this is an isolated 1950s tourist enclave of exclusive
interest to divers. The hotel is adequate but the diving is superb. Lots
of activities. 77 rooms and 24 bungalows.

## CAYO LARGO

**Sol Pelícano $$$$** *tel: (45) 248 333,* www.solmeliacuba.com. All the
hotels on Cayo Largo del Sur are all-inclusive, booked as packages
from abroad. This 4-star hotel has all the facilities you could possibly
need for a successful beach holiday, offering activities such as div-
ing and lots of entertainment for children. 307 modern, functional
rooms and junior suites.

## MATANZAS PROVINCE

## VARADERO

**Meliá Las Américas $$$–$$$$** *Carretera Las Morlas, Playa Las
Américas, tel: (45) 667 600,* www.lmeliacuba.com. This swanky
5-star hotel is a highly-ranked all-inclusive golf and beach re-
sort offering international quality and facilities. Adults only. 332
rooms and suites.

**Meliá Varadero $$$$** *Autopista del Sur, Playa Las Américas, tel: (45)
667 013,* www.meliacuba.com. Located next to the Plaza Las Ameri-
cas Convention Center and Shopping Center and the Varadero Golf
Club. This is an all-inclusive mega-complex with tons of amenities:
fountain, pool, five restaurants, disco, shops and more. Direct beach
access. 490 rooms.

**Mercure Cuatro Palmas Varadero $$–$$$** *Avenida 1ra e/ 60 y
64, tel: (45) 667 040,* www.accorhotels.com. An attractive beachside
complex on either side of the road of colonial-style villas and bunga-
lows. Some of the rooms (which can be a little worn) are arranged

around an excellent pool. 282 rooms with air conditioning. Convenient for down town, nightlife and restaurants.

## ZAPATA PENINSULA

**Villa Guamá $** *Laguna del Tesoro, Ciénaga de Zapata, tel: (45) 915 991*, www.hotelescubanacan.com. Reached by boat, this is one of the most distinctive places to stay in Cuba with replica Taíno village. Thatched huts are spread over interconnected islands in the middle of a swamp. Mosquito repellent essential. Good for birdwatching Crocodile on the menu.

## CENTRAL CUBA

## CIENFUEGOS

**La Unión $$–$$$** *Ave 31 esq. 54, tel: (43) 551 020*, www.hotelescubanacan.com. The building dates from 1869 and has been restored into a hotel, making this one of the nicest places to stay in the area, but its town centre location means it can be noisy. Facilities include a business centre, gym, courtyard, pool (which can get very crowded), car rental, restaurant and bars.

## TRINIDAD

**Iberostar Grand Hotel Trinidad $$–$$$** *José Martí 262 y Lino Pérez, tel: (41) 996 070*, www.iberostar.com. Centrally located, this is the best hotel in the area. Good service, good food, lovely renovated old building. 40 rooms, some with balconies overlooking the plaza, but no pool or terrace.

## CAYO COCO

**Tryp Cayo Coco $$$** *Cayo Coco, tel: (33) 301 300*, www.meliacuba.com. One of Cuba's most attractive resort hotels, a replica of a colonial village amid palm gardens and by a dazzling white beach. Pastel-coloured villas interwoven by a magnificent sculpted pool. Watersports, diving centre, restaurants, shops. 508 rooms.

## CAYO GUILLERMO

**Iberostar Daiquirí $$$** *Cayo Guillermo, tel: (33) 301 650,* www. iberostar.com. A good, popular, all-inclusive family hotel, with bright, recently refurbished rooms, each with its own balcony. Long, narrow beach, shallow sea. Good food, buffet or themed restaurants, nice pool, excellent service. 312 rooms.

## CAMAGÜEY

**Gran Hotel $–$$** *Calle Maceo, 67, tel: (32) 292 094,* www.islazul.cu. This colonial building in the heart of town has been a hotel since 1939. Handsome lobby, pleasant piano bar and nice suites. Most rooms have balconies, but those overlooking the street can be noisy. 72 rooms.

## PLAYA SANTA LUCÍA

**Club Amigo Caracol $$–$$$** *Playa Santa Lucía, tel: (32) 365 158,* www.hotelescubanacan.com. The resort's prettiest hotel has flower gardens and two-storey villas with fancy bedrooms, each with balcony, sea view and sitting area. Lots of activities and facilities. 150 rooms.

### ORIENTE: THE EAST

## GUARDALAVACA

**Paradisus Río de Oro Resort and Spa $$$$** *Playa Esmeralda, tel: (24) 430 090,* www.meliacuba.com.com. This all-inclusive resort is the best in the area and one of the most luxurious hotels in Cuba, situated on a pretty bay. Four very good restaurants including Japanese and Creole.

## SANTIAGO DE CUBA

**Hotel Casa Granda $$$** *Heredia, 201 (on Parque Céspedes), tel: (22) 686 600/653 021,* www.gran-caribe.cu. A grand white building in the heart of Santiago, overlooking the main plaza, this classic hotel is a great place for people-watching, but the rooms are tired and dingy.

In its heyday Joe Louis and Graham Greene's 'Man in Havana' stayed here. Terrace bar with great views. 58 rooms.

**Hotel E San Basilio $–$$** *San Basilio 403 e/ Calvario y Carnicería, tel: (22) 651 702.* Central and convenient for shops and sites of interest, this boutique hotel is simple but charming. Restaurant, lobby bar, and only 8 rooms.

**Meliá Santiago de Cuba $$$–$$$$** *Av. de las Américas y Calle M, tel: (22) 687 070, www.meliacuba.com.* Santiago's most ostentatious hotel, 3km (2 miles) from the centre. Six bars, luxury pool, indulgent buffets and snazzy nightclub. 302 rooms.

## BARACOA

**Hotel El Castillo $–$$** *Calixto García, Loma del Paraíso, tel: (21) 645 106, www.grupo-gaviota.com.* One of Cuba's most charming hotels, converted from one of Baracoa's old forts. Perched on a cliff, it has a fine pool, gardens, mountain views, helpful staff and spacious bedrooms. A real bargain. 34 rooms.

**Hostal La Habanera $–$$** *Maceo 68 esq. Frank País, tel: (21) 645 273, www.grupo gaviota.com.* This pretty pink building in the town centre was converted to a hotel in 2003 and is designed on traditional lines with an internal courtyard and balconies. Small and stylish, it also has the best restaurant food in Baracoa. 10 rooms.

## CASAS PARTICULARES (PRIVATE LODGINGS)

## HAVANA

**Casa Federico $** *Cárcel 156 e/ San Lázaro y Prado, Old Havana, tel: (7) 861 7817,* email: llanesrenta@yahoo.es. Spacious rooms in an apartment just off the Malecón. Good breakfasts, the only drawback is the climb up the 64 stairs. Friendly and helpful hosts.

**Evora Rodríguez $** *Prado 20 e/. San Lázaro y Cárcel, Old Havana, tel: (7) 861 7932,* email: evorahabana@yahoo.com. Amazing apartment on ninth floor with tremendous views up the Prado and over the harbour to the fortresses. Huge rooms with large bathrooms, big windows open to sea breezes, making it light and airy. English spoken, good breakfast.

**Melba and Alberto** $ *Galiano 115, Apt 81, e/. Animas y Trocadero, Centro, tel: (7) 863 5178*, email: barracuda1752@yahoo.es. Rooms in an apartment on the eighth floor with great views from the balconies and worlds away from the down-at-heel street life of Centro. Comfortable rooms with use of kitchenette. Excellent meals offered.

## TRINIDAD

**Casa Colonial Muñoz** $ *José Martí, 401, e/ Fidel Claro y Santiago Escobar, tel: (41) 993 673*, www.casa.trinidadphoto.com. Colonial house built in 1800 with a shady patio and roof terrace, and large rooms furnished with antiques. Knowledgeable English-speaking hosts with children, their pet dogs and horse. One of the finest *casas* in Cuba. Horse riding can be arranged.

**Casa López-Santander** $ *Camilo Cienfuegos 313, e/ Jesús Menéndez y Julio Antonio Mella, tel: (41) 993 541*. Rooms in an attractive home dating from 1916, with a porch and striking neoclassical facade. Two blocks from Plaza Santa Ana; a 10-minute walk to the Plaza Mayor. Parking, and pleasant patio area.

**Hostal Isabel Cristina Prada** $ *Fernando Echerri 31, esq. Patricio Lumumba, tel: (41) 993 054*. A colonial house in the centre, near Plaza Mayor. One room has its own street entrance. It's in the main party street, though, so not so good if you want an early night.

## SANTIAGO DE CUBA

**Casa Colonial Maruchi** $ *San Félix 357 e/. San Germán y Trinidad, tel: (22) 620 767*, email: maruchib@yahoo.es. Ideal location in the heart of the old city, lovely colonial house around central courtyard garden. The two guest rooms have high ceilings, exposed timbers and contemporary décor. English spoken.

**Casa Colonial Tania $** *Santa Rita 101, e/ Padre Pico y Callejón Santiago, tel: (22) 624 490,* email: aquiles@cultstgo.cult.cu. Central yet quiet colonial house with high ceilings. Two rooms, each with bathroom, one double, one twin, fridge, air conditioning, terrace with harbour views. Meals available.

**Casa Dulce $** *San Basilio, 552, esq. Clarín, tel· (22) 625 479,* email: gdcastillo20@yahoo.es. Apartment upstairs on the corner, with large windows to catch the breeze. Comfortable room, charming English-speaking hostess, pleasant roof terrace; spectacular views of the city.

## VIÑALES

**Villa Los Pinos $** *Salvador Cisneros, 36, tel: (48) 796 097.* Colonial house built in 1892, on the main street. The bedroom has independent access, two double beds, air conditioning and a good bathroom. English and French spoken by knowledgeable couple.

## SANTA CLARA

**Casa Mercy $** San *Cristóbal 4 e/. Cuba y Colón, tel: (42) 216 941,* email: arnaldomm@uclv.edu.cu. Charming hosts offer two spacious rooms overlooking the street in this comfortable house which is very central. Pleasant roof terrace for cocktails, excellent food offered and any diet accommodated.

**Hostal Florida Center $** *Candelaria, 56 e/ Colon y Maceo, tel: (42) 208 161.* Colonial house on one level around a leafy courtyard. The charming host is an excellent cook. The rooms contain antique furniture but have modern luxuries as well.

## BARACOA

**Casa Colonial Lucy $** *Céspedes, 29 e/ Rubert López y Maceo, tel: (21) 643 548.* Pretty colonial house run by the efficient Lucy, who can arrange excursions and knows what is going on. Lovely rooms and a pleasant roof terrace with terrific views over the town to the sea. Good food available, local specialities served.

# INDEX

**Berlitz®** pocket guide

# Cuba

**Thirteenth Edition 2015**

**Written by** Fred Mawer
**Updated by** Maciej Zglinicki
**Edited by** Kate Drynan
**Cartography updated by** Carte
**Update Production:** AM Services
**Picture Editor:** Tom Smyth
**Production:** Rebeka Davies and Aga Bylica